# BUT NOW I SEE

*A Spiritual Awakening*

Prophetess Kayle Bryant

# Dedication

With the heart of honor and to whom honor is due, I wish to dedicate the book to Apostle Janice L. Dillard (my spiritual mother), who has immensely impacted my journey. You have been my true covering. You prayed for me and your prayers found me. I am so grateful that you've been a part of my life. If it had not been for you, I know I would have been dead. So thank you for being the shepherd over my soul throughout all of these years.

Thank you, Lord, for this spiritual mother who was sent as a cultivator and a prayer warrior. She has pioneered a way for the next generation of eagles to arrive and to fly.

# *Acknowledgments*

First, to Bishop Clarence Joseph Bryant. Not many can say they have a prophet, a prayer warrior, provider, protector, and a patient man of God in their life. I am so grateful for your love and support. You're my #1 fan and motivator. Love has always been what it does and I thank you for loving me through this process. I am forever yours.

Next…to my children, Markale and Imani: In the beginning, God created Heaven and Earth. It was His Grace that opened up Heaven's doors and allowed the two of you to be born to me. You have brought tears and joy, but I am proud to say that I was able to be a gate and gatekeeper to two of God's greatest investments. You are a blessing to hold and behold. The Bible declares in Acts 2:17, *And it shall come to pass in the last days, saith God, I will pour out my Spirit.* I pray that this book will bless you, my grandchildren, my great-grands, and generations to come. Mommy will forever love you.

To Gayle Saffeeulah. Our lives were not served on a golden platter. But God, in His infinite wisdom had His Hands upon us. Thanks for being an awesome and supportive little sister.

To my aunties, Daryl, Cathy, Marilyn, and Doris. When I moved in life, you all were always there. Love is the only word that can really describe aunts who have always felt like mothers. Thank you for your endless love and support. A family that prays together, stays together.

Prophetess Shantel Parris, you were always right, Prophetess! Special thanks for seeing what I could not see. And yes, let me re-introduce myself. From the Throne Room of Grace. A long push in a short time, my cousin-in-love.

To my BFFs, Taneshia Filmore and Cynthia Williams, who have shared prayers, tears, and years of friendship with me. There's a point in every true friendship where friends stop being friends and become sisters. I thank God for blessing me with the best friends...those who believed in me. Words cannot express the love we share.

Suprenia Santiago. You and I shall never part. Thank you for the dreams you dreamed that became reality and for the prayers you've prayed. Your love for me and your belief in me has been priceless. You are my sister forever.

# CHAPTER 1

There was an assassin in my life. An assassin who was waiting for me even before I was born. The assassin was there, but it was God who knew me. Jeremiah 29:11 says, *For I know the plans that I have for you, declares the Lord, plans for prosperity and not for disaster, to give you a future and a hope.*

God knowing me meant He knew everything about me. He knew of the greatness He'd instilled in me. He knew of the gifts He'd given to me. All that God had anointed me to be and all He anointed me to do was predestined before I left my mother's womb. So with that kind of greatness inside of me, it was no surprise that when I was born, an assassin was waiting to kill, steal, and destroy all the plans God had for me. The enemy was trying to make sure that I never reached my destiny.

My awareness of this attack happening in my life probably started when I was about five or six years old. Not that I understood everything that was going on, but I was smart enough to know that something wasn't right.

Growing up in a two-bedroom apartment in Pompano Beach, Florida, I was an only child, being raised by my mom after someone had shot my father. I was only eight years old when my father lost his life over a game of pool. The man who lost didn't want to pay my father, so he killed him.

I was told that my father's favorite color was white, and even though he was a brilliant gambler and a wise hustler, no one ever saw my father without his Bible. He knew the Lord, and my father also knew about the kingdom of darkness. However, my father's gifts didn't protect him from his destiny.

Of course, at such a young age, I wasn't aware of my gifts, but the assassin was *very* aware of God's plans for me. The assassin's attacks were subtle at first. I was just a child, so the assassin used the weapon that worked best on a child; the assassin used the fear that would naturally come to a child in the dark, at night in her room alone.

Inside my bedroom, I would lay in the darkness, tucked away in my bed as shadows moved around me and dark figures hovered above me. These weren't the normal shadows that children saw in the dark when light seeped into the room through an open door or streamed in from the outside through a window. No, these were real shapes of beings that I could see, and what was worse, I could feel. Every night, those shadows left me frozen with fear.

When I say frozen, I mean that. I was too afraid to move. The enemy had me captured, and I felt alone. I wasn't alone in my house; my mother was there, of course. However, there was no way I could jump out of bed and run to her. Even if I'd been able to find the courage to get up and run past the shadows, I wouldn't have been able to go to my mother. Although I always knew that she loved me, my mom was very strict; everything in our household had a time and place. At night, I had to be in bed at a certain time. If I wasn't, I'd be in trouble.

So I stayed in bed as the shadows and dark figures closed in around me. All I could do was cover my head with the blankets and pillows, trying to shield myself from the dark attacks that I felt coming. Closing my eyes and hiding my head were never enough to calm me. I would tremble with such terror that eventually, I'd just shake myself to sleep.

Night after night, I was terrorized and my fear led to another challenge for me—I became a bed wetter. There was nothing else I could do because once I was in the bed, I was too afraid to get up. Even if I had to go to the bathroom, I didn't move until the morning's early light would seep through my window.

I was a child, so I didn't yet know the power of God. I didn't know how to stand on the Word and declare 2 Timothy 1:7: *For God has not given us a spirit of timidity, but of power and love and discipline.*

That was the beginning for me and the assassin, although, again, I did not know what those dark shadows meant at that time. I didn't have anyone to talk to about this, no one could help me or even give me the protection I needed. Yes, my mother was there, but at that time in her life, she was a hustler. She was working hard, doing everything she could to give me a good life. She had a couple of jobs, working in the schools and as a bus driver. She did all of that to make sure I had the finest clothes, the latest toys, the best of everything.

However, with all my mother gave to me, she wasn't spiritually gifted. Although she came to grow in Christ in the latter years, she wasn't at that point. My mother didn't have the spiritual knowledge or the wisdom to help me, and because she didn't have the spiritual tools, she unknowingly became part of the assassin's plan. One thing I learned as I got older was that the assassin moved from person to person, using anyone in his path to get to me.

So in those early years of my life, he used my mother. He used her with her strict discipline to keep me in that spirit of fear so I would never get out of bed at night, even when I was scared. Then during the day, she kept me in line with her rules. Everything in my life had to be flawless. My mother dressed me well, in the best clothes, and my hair was always neat. I appeared to be the perfect little girl—but everything wasn't always what it seemed. When I was just seven, my mother taught me how to take care of our home. I learned how to cook and I could prepare any kind of dish from rice to fried chicken that was as good as any adult's. I learned to clean so well that anyone could eat straight off of our floors.

By the time I was ten years old, I could take care of a household as well as a grown woman, and when I came home from school, that's what I had to do. Since my mother was usually still out working, after school, before I did anything, I would do my chores—getting dinner started and cleaning the house. Then, I had to do my homework.

On one particular day when I got home, I turned on the TV and went into the kitchen to cook. In a skillet, I heated the oil before I put the potatoes on to make French fries. While that was cooking, I turned to my other chores, but then a few minutes later, I smelled something burning. When I ran to the kitchen, I screamed—the kitchen was bursting with flames! I tried to pour water on the fire, but that only made the fire get larger. I was only nine years old, but I was fighting those flames like a professional firefighter. I was so scared that my house was going to burn down and then, what would my mother do? What would she say?

When it became too much for me, I ran to a neighbor's house and she called 9-1-1 before she called my grandmother. When my grandmother got on the line, I pleaded with her, "Please tell my mom not to beat me."

I was so distraught, my grandmother had to calm me down. "Okay, Kayle, I'll tell her. She won't beat you."

I believed my grandmother would tell my mother that, but still, I prayed.

When my mother got home, she took one look at our apartment (which had damage but was still livable), and then she took another look at me. After a moment, she said, "If I hit you, I'll kill you."

Covered in all of that black soot, I guess I already looked bad enough, or maybe my grandmother had convinced my mother. All that mattered to me was that I would not get a beating. I sighed with relief.

I truly felt as if God delivered me that day from more than just that fire.

Even when I was outside playing, my perfection had to continue. The day I lost the bow my mom had put in my hair that morning was horrifying and terrifying. If I went home without that bow, I would be in such trouble. Once again, I was in such fear, I was so distraught that the teacher stopped everyone in the class from playing.

"All right," she said when she had everyone's attention, "we're going to all look around and help Kayle find her bow."

Minutes later, when someone found the missing bow, I was so relieved.

That was the perfection my mother demanded and had instilled inside of me. I couldn't make the mistakes that every kid made.

My mother's motivation for me to be this way wasn't all bad. She was part of a generation who wanted her child to be better and to have more than she did. She wanted the best for me and because of that, she demanded the best from me.

So any time I stepped out of line and away from my mother's expectations, she punished me. As an adult, I came to understand that not all of that was my mother. The assassin was using her as part of his plan.

Of course, as a child, I didn't have that kind of understanding. I just became this little fearful ten-year-old adult who tried to live life perfectly. I was a little girl walking alone and walking into the unknown. I didn't have any covering from my mother under the blood of Jesus. Even still, I had the Lord. He knew me. It was later in my life when I came to understand Hebrews 13:5 where the Lord said He would never desert me, He would never abandon me. I came to truly realize that no matter what was going on in my life, the Lord had me covered the whole time…even as a little girl.

# CHAPTER 2

The assassin had the ability to move from one person to another, which was one of the things that gave the assassin that power over me. Whenever I left home, the assassin was able to follow me; so I was never safe, not even at my school, not even in my classroom. The assassin was able to use kids against me.

Girls I knew and those I didn't would come up to me and say they wanted to fight me for no reason. This was something I never understood. I never bothered anyone; I certainly didn't start any trouble. I had to behave because of the fear I had of my mother. However, the assassin used these kids, without reason, to come after me so that I wouldn't have any peace.

Often I would run home in fear, but then, there were other times when I would stay and fight because I was afraid if I didn't, the harassment would never end. It was as if I was a magnet for bullies. Now, I know this was just another sign of the assassin.

Because of the way the assassin used other kids, I didn't have many friends my age. There wasn't much I was able to do after school with friends anyway, so I gravitated toward teachers. When I was a child, people always said that I had an old soul because I liked being around older people. I think it was just that I loved being surrounded by wisdom.

It wasn't all bad for me at school. When I was in pre-school, I was named Miss Markham Elementary. Even with all that was going on with me at home and with other little girls, I was crowned a little queen.

This is something that began at that time, but I experienced it all through my life. Even though the assassin was there, God always had a moment of glory or gave me a moment of honor. It didn't matter what was going on, God was always setting me up for greatness. He was allowing me to realize that I had His favor. But right after I was crowned the little queen, my mom pulled me out of that school and enrolled me at Charles Drew Elementary, which was closer to my grandmother's house. Life didn't change much for me at Charles Drew. Of course, there were girls there who wanted to fight me since the assassin followed me. At school, I had to fight. When I left school, I had to fight, even getting attacked on the school bus going home. Girls would come after me and the bus driver would say nothing. And then at home, I was still facing the darkness and the demons. I was fighting my way through more than just school, sometimes I felt like I was fighting my way through life.

Even with all of that, I began to make a few friends. At school, there was April, whose mother dressed her just like my mother dressed me: in Jordache, Sergio Valente, and Sassoon jeans. She also liked to dance, and what was best was that she didn't pay any attention to the girls who talked about me and bullied me.

Then there was my best friend, Annette. We didn't attend the same school, but we lived in the same building, which gave us a lot of time to spend together. She lived one floor beneath us and not only did we play outside together, but Annette was also the only kid my mother allowed in our apartment. My mother liked Annette so much that many nights when we sat down to dinner, Annette was right there with us. She was like a sister to me and was there, always by my side.

It didn't matter that I had friends, though. The assassin was always right there, ready to fulfill his goal to destroy me. It happened with just the smallest things. One day when I was playing in the apartment playground, Annette and I and a couple of other kids were just tossing rocks back and forth to each other. This was a game that we'd played before, but then all of a sudden, one of the rocks landed right in the middle of my head and split my forehead wide open! There was so much blood that my mother had to rush me to the hospital, where the doctor gave me stitches.

Another time, I was running home from school and slipped on the stairs, slashing the skin at the corner of my eye. It just seemed to never stop—the enemy was using everything against me; the name of the game was to take me out and there was nothing I could do about it.

As I said, I didn't have the spiritual awareness and I didn't have the prayers of my mother. The enemy knew that my mother and I were ignorant of his devices, so it was almost like he felt he had free rein.

Soon though, I began to grow in my walk with God and that's when things began to change.

# CHAPTER 3

One of my favorite parts of the week was when all of my cousins and I would go to my grandmother's house. Big Ma rounded up all of her grandkids, about ten of us, and we spent the weekend in her four-bedroom house. It didn't matter how many bedrooms there were—we all found somewhere to lay our heads. Those weekends were the best.

When I was in elementary school, Big Ma got married again and all of us were excited about it. Pop was the best step-grandfather. Not only was he always so nice, but he'd get out there and play with us. That made it even more fun to go to Big Ma's house.

Being there at my grandmother's house with Big Ma, Pop, and my cousins were the only times when I felt like I was truly a kid. Because I was an only child, I spent so much time alone at my house, especially as my mother worked. When Annette had to go home there were so many times when I was by myself. At my grandmother's house, though, it was like

I had a whole bunch of siblings. We were close in age and as tight as brothers and sisters.

I only saw my cousins at my grandmother's house. Even though we lived close, my cousins didn't like coming over to my house. My mother had given me all the games and gadgets, so whenever my cousins came over, we always had fun, but there was another side. My mother was just as strict with my cousins as she was with me and none of them liked that part. So, we spent most of our time together at grandmother's house.

While we always had a good time with my grandmother, she took her responsibility for us seriously. Not only did she take care of us and disciplined us when we needed it, but she also made sure that we were spiritually grounded.

That meant that on Sundays, Big Ma took us to church. All ten of us somehow crammed into Big Ma's green Chrysler and went to Apostolic Church of Jesus, an old-fashioned small church that had only about fifty members—and that was on a good Sunday. The size of the church didn't matter to Big Ma. She wanted to make sure that we were taught all of the basics of God: who He was, who Jesus was, the difference between heaven and hell.

In church, we didn't go much beyond those basics; we didn't go deep. The pastor didn't teach us about the spiritual realm and spiritual warfare. Back in those days, that wasn't something taught in church. That wasn't something that anyone ever spoke about. I'd heard of demons, but I didn't really know what that word meant and as a child, I wasn't making the connection between that and what I was going through with the assassin.

So even though I was in a spiritual battle, going to church didn't help me with the fight that I was in. At that time, I wasn't learning how to fight back against the assassin, but I was getting the foundation of learning who I would become in Christ and I would need that strong foundation.

I was ten years old when one day my mother told me she was pregnant. "You're going to have a baby?" I asked. I was so excited. The first thing I thought was that I wouldn't have to spend so much time by myself.

My excitement didn't last long, though, because then my mother said, "I'm not going to have this baby."

I couldn't believe it. I may have been only ten, but I certainly knew what that meant and I knew what an abortion was.

I begged my mother, "Please, Mom. Please." Right away, I began praying that my mom would not only have the baby but I would have a baby sister.

For days, I begged my mother and I prayed. I begged and prayed until my mother finally said, "Okay, but Kayle, listen, if I have this baby, it's yours."

That was fine with me. I was already operating so much as an adult that I agreed. "I'll do whatever you want me to do, Mom."

For the next months, I paid close attention to my mom, anticipating with excitement the arrival of my new baby sister. My mom continued to work, almost until the day my baby sister was born.

I was so excited when my grandmother came to get me while my mom went to the hospital to have her baby. Once the baby was born, my mother called me from the hospital.

She said, "Well, Kayle, I had this baby. Now, what do you want to name your baby?"

Her question surprised me. I knew she'd said that the baby would be mine, but I didn't think that meant that I would have to name the baby. I hadn't thought about that. A couple of seconds later, something came to me. I took the K off of my name and said, "Gayle. I want her name to be Gayle.

That was a proud moment for me. When Gayle came home, my mom put the baby in the room with me. From that day, with my mom's guidance, I raised my sister. It was a joy for me to help my mother do anything with Gayle, although I did begin to notice something that I hadn't expected. Ten years was a big difference in our ages at that point in our lives. We weren't going to be best friends—how could an infant be my best friend?

So the friends part didn't work out too well, but it was still wonderful to have a sister.

Once Gayle was born, except for school, no one ever saw me without my sister. From our house to the playground, to the church house, we were always together. I would even pick her up from the babysitter sometimes, and she was always with me when I spent the weekend with my grandmother.

On Sundays, we were still going to church and there was one particular Sunday when the presence of God was so evident during the service. I was only about twelve years old, but I began to hear the voice of God telling me to say something to the church. This was not a special service, not a Christian holiday. God just wanted me to stand up and let the church know that He was present and would be returning soon.

I listened to the voice of God and stood up. For the first time, I prophesied, telling the people that Jesus was coming back and He wanted us to worship Him and praise Him. Standing in front of those people and speaking those words felt totally natural to me; I'm sure my grandmother was surprised to see me and hear me, though, since I'd never done anything like that before. That was just another sign from God.

A few years later, things changed at Big Ma's house. Just like in every other part of my life, the assassin followed me, and this time, he used Pop.

It started one night when I was asleep in one of the back rooms. I'd been in a deep sleep, but suddenly, I felt something, a presence, and woke up. I couldn't see anything at first, but I knew that Pop was in the room. Right away, I felt fear, something I'd never felt with him before. This time, though, I wondered why he was in my room; I knew he wasn't supposed to be there.

I stayed as still as I could as I felt him walk closer and closer until he stood over me. Then, he leaned over and touched me.

He fondled me with his hands, but I stayed as still as a stone, too afraid to move, too afraid to do anything.

He only stayed for a few minutes before he turned and left. The moment he closed the door behind him, I jumped from the bed and ran to the bathroom. I cried so hard that night and then cried so many other nights when he did the same thing. Or, when he would come into the bathroom while I was taking a shower. I'd always enjoyed being with Big Ma, but now being at her house was sometimes like living a nightmare. Every creepy touch was a terrifying moment.

It was hard to believe that Pop was doing this. He'd been so nice to us; just like a grandfather. Everyone loved him. However, the man who'd been so nice, the man who I loved so much, kept doing it to me over and over. I never said anything because just like so many other times, the assassin used fear to lock me in and keep me silent. Now, not only was I afraid of the dark, but I was afraid to open my mouth and tell anyone.

Who would I tell anyway? Would anyone even believe me? And if they did believe me, I didn't want to hurt my grandmother. I knew if she found out what Pop was doing, she'd be so upset.

Lastly, I definitely couldn't tell my mother. One thing I knew for sure—she'd believe me, so I was afraid of what she'd do. My mother was a fighter and I had no doubt that if she found out what this man was doing to me, she would get her gun and kill him.

I didn't want to hurt Big Ma, I didn't want my mother to get in trouble, I didn't want to take the chance that no one (except for my mom) would believe me. So I stayed in the dark and I kept that dark secret because the assassin had instilled the spirit of fear inside of me from such an early age. Fear was a constant in my life, even though God never wanted me to have that spirit. This continued until I was about twelve years old and then, the anger of what Pop was doing began to build up inside of me. It wasn't just what he was doing, it was everyone. I was tired of being attacked, tired of fighting everybody. There was one assassin, but he was using so many people to get to me and I felt as if I was being locked down—locked down in my voice and locked down in my spirit.

That made me angry and courage began to build in me. I rebelled, found my voice, and stood up to Pop. Now, whenever he came up to me as I was in the kitchen washing dishes or something like that, I would push his hands away and whip around facing him.

I looked him straight in his eyes and told him, "If you touch me again, I'm gonna tell my grandmother." It was a threat, but I meant it. I was no longer willing to let him take advantage of me. Finding my voice helped a little bit. The fondling stopped, though Pop would still try to sneak a peek when I was in the bathroom or getting dressed. But at least I had stopped him from touching me. At least I had lived to fight another day.

The constant fighting was tough on me, especially since the assassin took on so many variations. Between my mom, the kids, and then Pop, that was enough. Then, the enemy began to even use my teachers. Some teachers thought I was a star pupil, and some teachers would accuse me of doing something, even if I was just sitting at my desk doing my work.

I always made sure I kept my grades up and my mother wasn't too concerned about that because she knew I'd do well. However, there was one thing that my mother never tolerated and that was a call from one of my teachers. That would be the reason for serious punishment.

It happened, though. A teacher called my mother telling her that I'd done something that I hadn't done. I was too afraid to misbehave in school. However, what I said didn't matter. My mother got that call, rushed over to my grandmother's house where I'd been staying, and started beating me with an extension cord. It was so bad that my grandmother had to jump in and stop her. The only way my grandmother got her to stop was to threaten to call the police.

That was a horrible moment for me. I was being punished for something I hadn't done. It was just another attempt by the assassin. The enemy was going to use everyone and everything to take me all the way out.

Not too long after that incident, though, life with my mother changed. When I was in middle school, my mom dedicated her life to Christ and once she had a personal relationship with God, she began to see me differently. She saw that God had His hands upon me. When she came to that understanding, our relationship changed. Rather than continuing to be so strict and such a disciplinarian, she began to walk in humility as it pertained to me. With that change, all of the beatings went away. That gave my mother and me a chance to become closer.

# CHAPTER 4

By the time I got to high school, the assassin had been attacking me for years and there were times when I felt so beaten down. While I had been venturing out and had more friends, the assassin was still using people to attack me. Even in high school, there were always two or three girls the enemy would use to come after me. They weren't challenging me to fights anymore, but they were still harassing me about everything from my hair weaves (extensions weren't popular at the time) to the designer clothes I wore.

It was the spirit of jealousy that continued to follow me, but it didn't bother me because I knew by then that I was different. Besides all of the superficial reasons the girls had for not liking me, I was mature and a lot wiser than my age.

I didn't talk like them, I didn't think like them, I didn't dress like them and it didn't bother me at all—God had made me this way, just a little different. He had set me apart.

The few friends I did have in high school always defended me, encouraged me, and reminded me that this was nothing but the spirit of jealousy. LaShunna was the one who was always by my side telling me this.

"Just remember, Kayle, people have been jealous of you your whole life. Don't pay them any mind."

LaShunna understood. We'd had many talks about how we grew up and we had a couple of things in common. Her father was an attorney and her parents had given her the finer things in life as well. Some girls had been jealous of her, too, so I listened to what she said. Often, I gleaned off of her self-esteem; we were good for each other.

However, I also knew that what I experienced with these girls wasn't just jealousy. The assassin was still very much in my life and it was in high school when I discovered that the assassin wasn't just trying to destroy me, the enemy really was out to kill me.

In the tenth grade, I got my first job at Kentucky Fried Chicken. I was so excited; I was on my way to being independent and having a little of my own money. But just like with everything in my life, the assassin followed me to work.

On my first day, the manager introduced me to everyone and then trained me. As he was working with me, I saw one of the girls standing off to the side, just staring at me. I didn't know her, but I recognized that look and I knew it was trouble. All I could do was ignore her.

For three days, everything stayed the same—I went to work, the girl glared at me, and I just did my job, doing everything I could to ignore her. Finally, she spoke her first words to me: "I'm gonna get you."

I didn't respond to her; all I did was shake my head. This story never changed and it seemed like it was never going to end. At least we were in high school, so she wouldn't want to fight. The assassin was just using her; she was just talking.

That day when I left work, I stood outside KFC waiting for my mom to pick me up. Usually, she was there when I got off, but on that day, she was running late. As I stood there, a car swerved into the parking lot and before I could make sense of what was happening, the car screeched to a stop right in front of me. The girl who worked with me jumped out of the front passenger seat with a razor blade in her hand. There was hardly a way for me to protect myself because she came at me so fast and once she slashed my face with that razor, I was down.

I screamed and tried to fight back, but I felt weak from the slash on my face. I felt the strength fading from my body, but then all of a sudden with a power I didn't know I had, I grabbed her and threw her up against the brick wall, right when people came running out of the restaurant.

She wrestled free from me and then jumped back into the car. It sped away as one of the people yelled, "Call nine-one-one. She's bleeding!"

When I heard that, I felt the blood pouring from my face and dripping onto my shirt. I began crying profusely. Why had she done that? I didn't even know her name and I doubted that she knew mine. But it was the assassin coming to kill me.

The paramedics arrived, but I didn't want to go with them. Instead, I called my Aunt Gail because I figured if my mom wasn't there by then, she was out, still working. My aunt rushed to KFC, got me into her car, and we sped to North Broward Hospital.

After the doctors examined me, I discovered that it wasn't just my face that had been slashed, I'd been stabbed in my side. The deep cut on my face required eleven stitches, and I needed twenty-two stitches in my side. By the time I was ready to be released, my mom had come to the hospital. She'd been so worried when she'd heard I'd been attacked and when I told her what happened, she was even more upset with the girl.

Still, my mother said, "Kayle, you've got to be doing something to these girls. You've got to be starting something. Why are these girls just always bothering you?"

My mother had been saying that to me since I was in elementary school. Whenever I came home and told her that some girl didn't like me or some girl wanted to fight me, she asked what was I doing to them. It wasn't that my mother thought I was out there creating trouble. It was just that she couldn't understand why so many girls didn't like me.

There was no way for me to get her to understand that I didn't have anything to do with this…it was all the assassin. Demons were hanging on to my destiny and that meant I would always be a target for the enemy.

Of course, I wanted to get revenge on the girl I worked with, but not only did I come from a Christian family, but *I* was also a Christian, too. So going back to fight like that wasn't an option. My option was to pray.

I didn't return to that job, although I could have. The girl who attacked me was expelled from our high school because of what she'd done and she was assigned to an alternative school. She didn't return to school until about a year later.

A few weeks after I'd been attacked, I was at a prayer meeting at my grandmother's house, and my cousin, Prophetess Verdie Mae Wilkes, was there as well. I'm blessed to be from a family filled with prophets, prophetesses, evangelists, and teachers and after the meeting ended, my cousin came straight over to me.

She stared at me for a moment before she said, "I know you want revenge, but God's got you. The enemy came to kill, but when that girl went to hit you, it was an angel who threw her against the wall. That blade that stabbed you was supposed to cut open your lungs. But she could not kill you. Don't worry about the revenge," the prophetess told me. "God is going to take care of it."

I wanted to rejoice. Before my cousin said this, I had not understood how I'd thrown that girl against the wall. Now I knew angels were fighting for me. It made sense; now that I was older, I had some kind of understanding of what was happening to me. I knew about the black spirits from discussions I'd heard in my family. I didn't know much about them; I didn't know their characteristics or how they operated. But slowly, I was coming into this knowledge and understanding. Satan didn't like me, and now I knew that he was really out to kill me.

By this point in my life, I had become comfortable, in a way, with the assassin. He had been there ever since I could remember and I had learned to live with him. I think also, I began to realize that like Job, the assassin had been able to come into my life, but the enemy would never be able to fully destroy me. The assassin, Satan, went to and fro, seeking to devour me, but the enemy wouldn't be able to touch the favor that God had given to me. God was the investor and I was His investment. There would always be a limit on what the assassin would be able to do to me because God protected His investments. Just like the Lord says in Matthew 28:20, *Behold, I am with you always, to the end of the age.*

With that understanding, I began to get out even more. I was still being rejected by a lot of girls, but now, I didn't let that hold me back. I became more social and started participating in clubs and groups in school. First, I joined the cheerleading team in high school and I remained on that team for the entire four years.

Next, I joined the chorus because again, my family was filled with gifted singers and blessed with beautiful voices. I never felt that I was anointed to sing since I'd always been a background singer, but being in the chorus allowed me to step out as a singer instead of hiding behind everyone else.

I loved being in the chorus because singing helped me to forget about the things that were happening to me: the abuse, the rejection. The chorus was a perfect outlet for me since I loved singing so much. My music teacher, Mr. Kenneth Howard, was able to nurture me and pull out all of my strengths. Even though he was stern like my mother, he was able to bring the beauty out in music. And I loved that.

There was another change for me in high school—I began dating. Marc was a senior and a football player and I was a cheerleader. Everything about him was wonderful to me: he was nice and kind, funny and loving. Whenever we were together, we had a good time, whether we were hanging out with friends or just with each other. My mother was still strict, but not when it came to me dating. There were some parts of my life where she left me alone, probably because she knew she had raised me well and she knew I'd always try to do the right thing. So my mother was never concerned about my behavior when it came to dating and she never asked about my grades when it came to school. She never asked about my report card, but she didn't have to; I did well in school. I had always been a good student because I knew my mother only expected the best from me.

For a while, being in high school was new and different, but the spirit of jealousy continued to follow me. I continued to find myself in the middle of drama with girls who didn't even know me. The years of these kinds of battles began to weigh down on me like a massive burden that had become too heavy for me to carry. I was weary—tired of the fear, tired of the fights with other girls, tired of being reared by a strict mother, tired of being molested by my step-grandfather. Although my mother wasn't as strict and my step-grandfather had backed off, I think I still carried the weight of all that had happened to me in the past. I'd been beaten down to a dark place; I was depressed.

By the time I got to the eleventh grade, I was so tired that I just wanted everything to end. No one thing in particular pushed me to this point; it truly was just the accumulation of the years of being in a battle. I was walking around functioning, but I was functionally depressed, able to operate under depression and oppression. At that point, I just wanted it to be over and decided to take my own life.

One night while I was home alone, I went into the medicine cabinet and got a whole bottle of pills—I'm not even sure what they were. I just knew there was enough in there for it to be over. I sat down on the bed, stared at the bottle for a few minutes before I swallowed every single pill. I felt nothing emotionally when I laid down and closed my eyes. All I expected was that when I opened my eyes, I'd be looking into the face of God.

But the next morning, my eyes opened and I was still in my bedroom. The only thing that was different was that I had a buzz in my ears that continued for hours. I didn't understand any of it. Why hadn't I died?

When the buzzing went on and on and on, I called one of my aunts in the medical field and I asked her, "What happens when someone takes a whole bunch of pills and they hear a buzz in their ears?"

"Oh, that's the brain responding to an overdose."

"Wow," was all I said before I thanked her and hung up. So, I *had* overdosed. But nothing happened. Why not? Why was I still here?

Even as I asked those questions in my mind, I knew the answers. I knew that I had the protection that I'd had all of my life. There were angels always beside me, fighting for me when I couldn't or wouldn't fight for myself. In my weakness, God proved Himself strong once again. His hand was upon my life. He stepped in and protected His investment just like He says in Psalm 34:18, *The Lord is near to the brokenhearted. And saves those who are crushed in spirit.* I was so valuable to God. When I couldn't tap into my self-worth, God had declared greatness over my destiny.

Even when I was willing to give in to the assassin, God wasn't going to allow the assassin to take me out, no matter the thoughts that got into my head.

In my latter years, I came to understand exactly what kind of protection I really did have in my life. I was God's creation, the apple of His eye. So whenever danger came, God sent the angels He'd assigned to me to help me to stand so that I could one day step into the greatness He had for me. With my suicide attempt, God was sending a message not only to the enemy but to me as well. God was saying that no matter what the assassin tried, he would never be successful. The assassin could try to give me a death sentence, but God would give me life. Whether the attempt to kill me came at the hands of someone like the girl at KFC or if I was trying to do it myself, God's protection was going to be there and death was not going to come prematurely to my door.

The scripture from Isaiah 54:17 says, *No weapon that is formed against thee shall prosper* was really my life. God may have allowed these attacks to form, but they were never going to prosper. The plans of the assassin would never come to be.

If I'd had that full understanding of God from the beginning, I would have also known that I was in a war—a spiritual war. In the book of Ephesians, God tells us that we're in a war, but it's no ordinary battle in Ephesians 6:12: *For our struggle is not against flesh and blood, but against the rulers, against the authorities, against the powers of this dark world and against the spiritual forces of evil in the heavenly realms.*

From the scripture, we see that we will face wars, but for us to be the victors, we have the know-how to fight these wars—they cannot be fought in the natural. To win these wars, we must understand that we're in a spiritual battle and that is the level where we have to fight.

I was in a spiritual war the moment I was born because the enemy recognized the gifts and calling upon my life. The greatness that God had instilled in me was the reason why the assassin wanted to destroy me. He didn't want those kinds of gifts in the world, so he studied my strengths and weaknesses to become familiar with the ways his attacks would be most effective.

Of course, as a child and even as a teen, I didn't know or understand this. I didn't have the knowledge and as God tells us in Hosea 4:6, *My people perish for lack of knowledge.* But as a child, I had no wisdom and since this was before my mother dedicated herself to the Lord, she couldn't help.

In the natural, I grew up without those safeguards and that was why the assassin was able to come after me freely. But the true battle wasn't in the natural and because God was my ultimate protection, the enemy could harass me, provoke me, persecute me, even torment me. But what the enemy could not do, was destroy me.

That didn't stop the assassin from trying, though. As I matured into adulthood and began to gain my own wisdom as I moved closer to Christ, the enemy realized he risked losing me altogether. So he had to try new tactics and he began to use spirits to come after me.

Over the years, I'd battled all kinds of spirits: the spirit of rejection, the spirit of anger, the spirit of fear, and when none of those worked to take me out, he ultimately sent the spirit of suicide—if he couldn't take me out himself, maybe he could put thoughts into my head so that I would do it for him. The assassin couldn't destroy me, but he could leave behind demons that manipulated my mind.

I had been in this invisible war, but I didn't want to fight because I was tired. The enemy made me believe that the only solution to everything I'd been through was to just end it all. At that time, I had even lost the ability to speak light into my life, even though all I had to do was quote God's word back to Him. The light I needed had already been written in the scriptures.

In Psalm 17:8, the scripture says, *Keep me as the apple of Your eye; Hide me in the shadow of Your wings.*

All of my life, I'd been hidden in the shadow of the Lord's wings. I'd been protected, I had God's favor. With His favor, He had given me everything that I would need to accomplish the purpose He had for my life. When I came to that understanding, I truly began to realize all that God had given to me. Some talents and gifts, I'd taken for granted. For instance, I'd always been gifted with my hands. From cooking to cleaning, I could run a household. And then, I'd learned from my mom (who was gifted in hairstyling) how to do hair like an adult. God had blessed me with all of these things and now that I recognized that, I was determined to do a few things: 1) I was not going to allow the enemy to trick my mind again and try to take me out, 2) I was going to recognize all that God had given to me, and 3) I was determined to use every talent and gift that He had blessed me with because I finally understood I had a purpose and I wanted to become the woman God wanted me to be.

# CHAPTER 5

At the beginning of my senior year in high school, I began thinking about something that seemed a bit out of my character—I considered running for Miss Ely High School. This might seem strange since I didn't have a lot of friends, but with all the activities I was involved in, I was a bit more popular than I had ever been.

When I told my friends I was considering this, they encouraged me. Even my first cousin, Dwayne, who was in the same grade as me told me I'd have his vote. Since I had everyone, including Marc (who had already graduated), on my side, I decided to do it. There were four or five of us running for the crown and we all had to prepare speeches to present to the student body.

On the day of our presentation to the senior class, I sat in the front row of the auditorium waiting my turn. Since my last name was Washington, I had to sit through the other speeches. Sitting and waiting wasn't a good thing; that only made me more nervous and gave me time to think. While there had been so many who encouraged me to do this, there were just as many, maybe even more who considered themselves my enemies. That jealousy spirit was rampant in the Senior class and I hadn't really considered that until this moment. As I waited I didn't know what was going to happen.

As each girl went up, she was received well, especially Lisa Thomason, who rapped. She was very popular as the Vice President of the class. The audience went into an uproar, cheering and applauding for her. Her good performance and the way she was received, encouraged me. Yeah, some people didn't like me, but I still had some friends in the auditorium. I tried to give myself a pep talk, but I was still a bit wary. I never knew when the assassin was going to show up, so my mind was set on ready-set-go mode, in case I had to get up out of there.

I wasn't concerned about my performance. I had confidence in what I was going to say and my ability to speak, but as the third girl went up, I began to shake. That spirit of fear covered me, so I began to pray.

Finally, it was my turn. I stood, walked across the stage, and stopped in front of the podium. It was silent as I looked out to the Senior class, and then the booing and heckling began. Before I'd even said a word, the enemy was attacking me. The teachers tried to calm the crowd as many in the auditorium shouted out to me.

"We don't want her!"

"Weavehead!"

"Get off the stage."

Even though I knew this was nothing but the enemy, it was still hard for me to stand there and listen to all of the hate for a good three minutes. Their words overrode all of my positive thoughts, so when the teachers finally got the students to calm down, I only had one thing to say.

I took a deep breath, then began, "For those of you who came to hear my speech, I'm so sorry. And for those of you who don't want to hear my speech, I'm sorry as well. But for those of you who will, vote for Kayle Washington for Miss Ely."

With that, I walked off the stage and the booing began again. They were so loud and rowdy, the teachers couldn't even get them under control this time. I had prayed that this wouldn't happen, but my prayers weren't enough. I was so humiliated that when I hit the door, I just ran.

Dwayne ran behind me, calling my name, but I didn't stop. I didn't stop until I got into the girls' bathroom because I wanted to be alone. I didn't expect Dwayne to follow me straight in there.

I leaned against the sink and just cried and cried.

"Don't cry," Dwayne kept saying, trying to console me. "It doesn't matter. If no one else votes for you, you've got my vote."

No matter what my cousin said, I was inconsolable. Finally, though, I was able to get myself together enough to have the nerve to leave the bathroom and head home.

That night, I called my cheerleading coach, who was also an advisor for the student council. I didn't want to make this call, but I needed to tell her what I'd decided to do.

"Please take my name off. I'm dropping out and I won't be running for Miss Ely."

"No, Kayle," she said. "I'm not taking your name off. You're not dropping out; you're going to run for Miss Ely."

What was my coach talking about? Didn't she see what had happened to me that afternoon? How could I run now after I'd been embarrassed that way?

"Who's going to vote for me?" I cried.

She said, "It doesn't matter. Even if the seniors don't vote for you, you have the juniors and sophomores and you have four hundred freshmen who just came to this school. All of them need to hear what you have to say."

I didn't care what my coach said. I just told her I wanted my name off the list!

"With all of those freshmen," my coach continued, "it won't matter who votes for you in any of the other classes. You get the freshman, and you will win."

The more I listened, the more encouraging her words became. Still, I felt so broken and very much embarrassed. I just couldn't do it.

No matter what I said, my coach wasn't trying to hear it. She wouldn't take my name off the list of Miss Ely candidates. "You'll be there," she said.

Eventually, she convinced me to stay in the race, but I can't say I felt better about it. When my mom came home that evening, I didn't even tell her what happened. I knew she would be supportive, but I also knew that she would ask me the same question she always did—what are you doing, Kayle, to make girls treat you this way?

I had never been able to get my mother to understand that it wasn't me...it was the light that people saw inside of me that they were reacting to. It was the light inside of me that the assassin wanted to put out.

With the encouragement of my cousin and coach, I was going to get back on that stage the next day to present my speech to the freshman class. This time, though, I was going to have a plan. The next morning, I had a picture of myself copied four hundred times and attached a piece of candy to each of the papers. Then, as the freshman class came into the auditorium to hear the speeches, I gave them my picture and a piece of candy.

Again, as I waited through the other girls' speeches, fear gripped me. Again, Lisa Thomason rapped, and like the seniors, the freshman loved her, turning that auditorium into an uproar.

When it was my turn, I walked up to the stage and looked out at everyone. I had a speech planned, but that's not what came out. It was almost like God put the *right* words in my mouth for that moment.

"Do you want your Miss Ely to have style?"

The auditorium exploded with, "Yes!"

I continued with my call and response presentation, asking those kinds of questions. The freshmen were into everything I was saying. In the end, I said, "Then, vote for Kayle Washington for Miss Ely," and walked off the stage feeling totally empowered.

The freshman set it off! They loved it, I had done it, and the same thing happened when I spoke before the sophomore and junior classes. I had come back from the depths of my embarrassment. God had given me favor.

That evening, at home, I got a call from our student president. Corey said, "Kayle, no one knows yet, but I want to tell you, you better have the best dress I've ever seen you wear because you just won Miss Ely!"

God had really turned this around. He had taken my embarrassment and humility and had given me honor. It was amazing what God had done for me and through me. I had been ready to give up, but God hadn't given up on me and He wasn't going to allow me to do that.

I'd gone from humiliation to being crowned the queen of my high school. It was such a significant prize and was the first time in my life when I fought back and the assassin was clearly defeated.

# CHAPTER 6

I graduated from high school in 1989 and at the time, my mother didn't want me to go to college. It wasn't that she didn't want me to do well in life; as I said, by this point, my mother recognized the gifts and talents that God had given to me. It was because of these gifts that my mother didn't believe college was necessary for me.

My mother had another reason, too—she wasn't excited about me leaving home. My mother had always tried to do the best she could for me and over the years, we'd gotten closer. Plus, I did so much at home; I basically took care of the house and I really took care of my sister. I think my mother feared losing me.

But even though Marc and I were so close now that I knew we would get married, I still wanted to go away to college. Not only did I want to further my education, but I wanted to get out of Florida. So many bad things had happened to me there, and I was under the false assumption that not only could I leave all of that behind, but maybe the assassin would stay behind, too.

I filled out all of the paperwork for several colleges and forged my mother's name. It was easy enough; my signature was already almost identical to my mom's.

My number one choice was Dillard University in New Orleans. It was interesting—out of all the states in this country, I wanted to go to Louisiana and New Orleans, specifically. When I was accepted, I was excited about going to an HBCU and I felt like New Orleans was the perfect place to run away to. Maybe in Louisiana, my life would change. I was so happy about the new possibilities.

What I didn't realize at the time was that all of the same problems, circumstances, and situations would follow me because the issues had been assigned to me. The assassin wasn't going anywhere; he was going to be right there in my life.

Once I told my mom I'd been accepted to Dillard, she asked me why didn't I just go to beauty school.

"Kayle," she said, "you're gifted with your hands, you do hair well, I think you would be fine just going to beauty school."

I told her that I just had to go, I had to get away. I really thought being 'out there' was the key to my happiness. The reality, however, was that I hadn't tapped into who I was and I wasn't recognizing who I belonged to. I had it in my mind that my destiny was out there waiting for me, not realizing that the greatness was inside of me. I was searching on the outside for what was already inside of me. I just didn't know it then, and I hoped to find what I was searching for at college.

When my mom finally accepted that I was going away, she rented a car and she and Gayle drove me to New Orleans. Within minutes of arriving on the campus, I met my roommate, but right away, I knew we weren't going to be close friends. She was quiet and withdrawn, and even though I had my walls up because of my past experiences with girls, I wanted to talk and be friends. But we were complete opposites.

Still, I was excited about the opportunity before me and I turned my attention to my academics. I'd decided to major in news broadcasting. I'd always admired the men and women who anchored the television news and I felt as if that was what God had predestined me to do.

After a couple of days at Dillard, I met Kashenia and Decole who were freshmen in my dorm as well. They were both from Dallas and it didn't take us long to really hit it off. They reminded me of my high school friends and the three of us hung out together all the time.

After a few weeks in school, though, something felt different. When I was in high school, I was a good student, never getting anything less than a B because I was always focused on what I had to do academically. However, at Dillard, I couldn't function in the same way. In the beginning, I couldn't even get my class schedule together. It took weeks to get that settled. Then, once I had my class schedule, I had a challenge with my classes. First, I was constantly waking up late, and even when I got to the class, I wasn't able to comprehend what the professors were saying. I couldn't think, I couldn't work, I was overwhelmed by all of the schoolwork. There were times when I just wanted to give up because I had no interest. I'd arrived at Dillard whole, but once there, I couldn't function mentally or emotionally. It didn't make sense; I couldn't explain what was happening. It was not only confusing, but it was completely out of control.

Even though I'd been through so much in my life, I was still ignorant of all the elements of spiritual warfare. So, I wasn't aware of the darkness in this city. I wasn't aware of all of the forces working against me. The assassin had followed me and this time, the enemy was using my youth and my first taste of freedom living away from home against me.

I may not have been able to focus in class, but I was always ready to hang out with Kashenia and Decole. We were first-year college kids away from home, so we did what freshmen did—we hung out, partied, and went drinking. Now, I had never been a drinker before, but when I hung out with them, we'd hop to different clubs and drink a whole bottle of MD **20/20** (often called by its nickname Mad Dog)— every college kid's favorite drink. But here was the thing—no matter how much I drank, I never got drunk. My girls would always get drunk, but the grace allowed me to be with my friends, and even though I wanted to be drunk like them, it never happened. No matter what the drink was, my body would never absorb it.

There were times when I felt like the oddball who couldn't get drunk. I had fun when we went out, but I wasn't like my friends. Kashenia and Decole had been out in the world much more than I'd been. Yes, Marc and I were in a relationship (in fact, now, we were engaged) but we didn't do all of that drinking and smoking and hanging out.

Even my conversation wasn't like everyone else's. I didn't go to New Orleans fluent in curse words. It was difficult for me to fit in with the crowd that way because those words weren't part of my language. I hadn't hung out the way they did, I didn't smoke the way they did. However, even with all of that, I was drawn to that crowd. I wanted to be like them, even as God was protecting me from that life.

God's angels never left me. One night, we were sitting around the dorm, and Kashenia, Decole, and I decided to get something to eat. Kashenia and Decole rode together and I followed them in my car.

We were on the highway, when they made a turn, I checked my mirror to make the same turn and I thought the coast was clear. But the moment I turned, another car crashed into my car, sending me spinning into the air. It happened so fast, but one thing I was sure of—my car was headed into the lake.

That didn't happen. I didn't hit the lake; I didn't even hit the median. The angel of God held up my car and prevented it from being damaged to the point where I would be hurt. When the car came to a halt, it was right on the edge of the lake and it was severely damaged, but I pushed the driver's door open, got out, and walked away without a scratch. Once again, God spared my life with His saving Hands on me. Like Psalm 121:3 says, *He who watches over you will not slumber.* God was never asleep. He wasn't like a man who needed to take a break; He was always on the job taking care of and protecting me, even when I was far away from home and acting just like a college kid.

Things didn't get better for me in the second semester of my freshman year. I was still struggling academically, but my social life was fine. Kashenia and Decole had started dating these two guys and whenever the guys came around, they usually brought a friend with them, a gentleman named Curtis.

When Curtis came with them, he would try to talk to me, but I wasn't interested. That didn't seem to matter to Curtis; he would always try. He never pressed me or anything, but I could tell he liked me.

I kept our conversations on the surface, just saying hello, asking how he was doing, that was pretty much it. Truly, we never did anything else or had a deeper conversation.

One day, Kashenia, Decole, the guys, and I drove out

to one of the lakes where all the kids and college students from the city hung out. There were always hundreds of kids gathering there.

When we arrived, we did what we always did—we found a place to sit and just hang out and talk. While we were sitting there, out of the corner of my eye, I saw this really tall girl start walking toward us. As she got closer, I could tell that something was up; she hadn't even said anything.

*Here we go*, I thought. I'd seen this look on so many girls for so many years of my life. I didn't know her and she didn't know me, but I could tell this was going to turn into a thing.

In the couple of seconds it took for her to get to me, I thought about the fact that I was in college and this was still happening. It was repetition from elementary school, to middle school and then high school. I thought I had left it behind there, but I guessed not—the spirit of jealousy followed me everywhere.

The girl walked up and didn't stop until she was all in my face. She confronted me…about Curtis.

"Are you dating Curtis?" she asked me.

Was she kidding? I hardly spoke to him. "Oh, no," I told her. "Kayle don't like Curtis, but I do know that Curtis likes Kayle."

Straight out of nowhere, she leaned back and punched me right in my face. Then, the fists started flying. Just like that, I had to flip and fight for my life. The fight went on for a couple of minutes before anyone came to break us up.

When some of the guys pulled us apart, I couldn't believe that my girls hadn't even jumped in to help me and I began to question if I had any friends in New Orleans. I was so angry when I turned away from everyone. The girl followed me and before I could get into my car and drive away, she threw a daiquiri all over my car. I couldn't believe it. Here I was in college and I still had to deal with this drama.

I had been back at the dorm for a little under an hour when my friends came back. They hadn't jumped in to help me, but they sure had a story to tell.

"You know, what Boss," one of my girls said to me, "you held your ground."

"Yeah," the other one said. "That girl was so big, but you pretty much won the fight."

They talked like they were excited, but I wasn't interested in hearing an account of the fight. I didn't care how the fight went. All I cared about was what I found out that day—I was pretty much alone.

Feeling that way didn't stop me from hanging out with them, though. When it was time for the next party, I was ready to go. This time, we were going to a club because we'd heard a lot of the New Orleans Saints would be hanging out there.

That sounded exciting to me, but then, by the time we got there, I once again felt like the odd girl out at the party. Like just whenever we went out, my girls had hooked up with someone and they had all scattered around the club. So, I was left sitting alone at the bar.

I must've looked so sad to anyone who noticed me as I sat there and kept asking myself, *What is wrong with me?* Guys would pass by or even stop to order a drink and it was almost as if I wasn't even sitting there. No one said hello, no one even looked at me.

I was trying to be part of this crowd, but what I didn't realize at the time was that I would never be. No matter what I tried to do, I couldn't change the fact that I'd been set apart for His glory. I was never meant to fit in; God had created me to stand out.

That night, I sat there alone for what felt like hours before the bartender asked me, "Hey, what would you like to drink?"

"Oh no. I don't want anything, thank you," I said.

Then, he said to me, "I know why no one is talking to you."

I looked up at him, I'm sure with a frown.

He continued, "You really do look like a woman who's already being taken care of. You don't look like you need anything. A man takes one look at you and he knows you already have a man. You don't look like you need a thing."

When I realized he was done, I didn't know what he wanted me to say. So I said, "Okay, thank you."

I really didn't want to talk; I was upset that I was sitting there by myself when my girls were off having a good time. Now, this bartender was telling me why I was alone. A few hours later, I left and went back to campus. I wasn't sure if my girls had left already or what, but I knew it was time for me to go.

We went back to that club a few times. *Secrets* was the place to be, but just about every time we were there, it was the same thing. My friends would be off having a good time and I would be left alone, secluded, and although I didn't realize it at the time, I was protected.

One night, as I was sitting at the bar, the owner of the club began to talk to me and that became my routine every time we went back there. My girls would go off and I would talk to the owner. I enjoyed hanging out with him. It wasn't that our conversation was all that great, but at least someone was talking to me.

After we'd been talking for a while, one night he asked me to go home with him. "I live right next door," he said.

"Okay," I said, without hesitation. I wasn't sure why I agreed to go with a guy I really didn't know, but I felt comfortable enough to do it.

He really did live close, right next door and upstairs from the club. When we walked into his small apartment, he put on some music. We sat on the sofa, playing with his puppy and just talking the way we had talked at the club. I wasn't nervous or worried in any way. I felt peaceful.

After we'd been talking for a while, he got up and went outside on his balcony. He didn't ask me to join him; I wasn't sure if it was because he went out there to smoke or what—I didn't ask him. I just stayed inside, still playing with the puppy.

When he came back inside, he sat next to me. He was quiet for a couple of moments before he said, "You know you don't have any friends here."

I frowned. "What do you mean?"

"The girls you hang out with are not your friends." I didn't say anything and he continued, "I can get a girl from anywhere. But a girl like you," he paused and shook his head, "I need to take you back to school because you don't belong out here. You don't belong here with me. You need to go back to the school and stay there."

His words surprised me. I thought, *What kind of guy is this?*

He didn't say anything else. He just got up and I stood and followed him. He still didn't say anything when we got into the car and when he dropped me off at school, that was the end of our relationship.

That was a shock to me that night, but later, I understood that it was all about the angels that had been assigned to me. The angels surrounding me had spoken to the demons inside that guy. My angels literally said to them, *No, you cannot touch her. Don't put your hands on her at all.*

No matter how many bad situations I allowed myself to be in, God was always looking out for me. He knew that I was surrounded by the kingdom of darkness, but by any means necessary, He was going to protect His investment because He had set me up to do great things in the kingdom.

There was nothing I could do to mess with His plans and my purpose.

# CHAPTER 7

When the school term ended, I went home, grateful to have the summer break. At home, I was able to find a summer job as a transporter in the local hospital. It was a simple job; all I had to do was transport patients from their rooms down to radiology for tests or X-rays. While I was working there, I met a guy named Norbert, who was a receptionist in that area. Every time I took a patient down to that floor, Norbert was there and he and I would say hi to each other. That was the extent of our friendship. I never really stopped to talk to him or anything.

I may have stayed away from talking to him because most mornings, he was always talking to another woman. After all I'd been through in my life with other females, I was wary. So, I always spoke to both of them, saying good morning. But that was it. I kept it moving. This went on for the entire summer and when I left the job to return to school, I didn't think any more about my summer job.

The week after I returned to campus, I got a phone call from an unfamiliar number. But since it was a 954 area code—from Florida—I answered.

After I said hello, the voice said, "Hi Kayle, this is Rose." I didn't recognize her name or her voice and I guess because I was quiet, she said, "You remember me. I worked at the hospital down near the radiologist."

"Oh," I said, surprised. "Hi, Rose." I had no idea why she was calling me. This was the first time I'd even heard her name. So I asked her, "How can I help you?"

Rose said, "Norbert told me all about how much you care for me, how much you love me."

I had no idea what she was talking about. First of all, I had never said anything to Norbert about her, and second of all, she was a female. Why would I be saying that I loved her?

"I don't know what you mean," I said to Rose.

She chuckled a little. "It's okay. I completely understand because I've been where you are. But you can come out the closet."

What was she talking about? "I'm sorry, Rose, but I'm not gay."

She kept talking as if she didn't hear me or believe me. "You know what? I used to fight it, too. But when you come out of the closet, you'll feel so free. And I already know," she insisted. "Norbert already told me how much you love me."

I couldn't believe she was saying this. "I'm so sorry. I don't know why Norbert lied to you. And you do know that I have a boyfriend, right?"

"You know what, Kayle? You'll get over it and when you're ready, we'll talk."

"Rose, I don't know how you got my phone number...."

Rose kept on talking and my roommate looked at me with a confused expression. I held my hand over the phone's speaker and said, "This lady thinks I'm gay." As Rose kept talking, I told my roommate that Rose would not take the truth for an answer. She was adamant, believing Norbert over me.

After listening to her for a few minutes, I realized that this was the assassin sending someone else after me with a new tactic. Based on someone else's lie, I was now in the middle of this.

Finally, I said to Rose, "Why don't you get Norbert on the phone? We'll both speak to him and find out why he lied to you." It took a while, but finally, Rose hung up. I really, really thought that was going to be the end of it, but then, not long after, Rose called back...with Norbert on the line!

I didn't want this drama but I was glad he was on the phone. At least with all three of us on the line, he'd have to tell her the truth. So with Rose listening, I asked Norbert, "Why did you lie to Rose?"

He said, "What are you talking about? You told me that every morning, you told me that all day. I didn't lie to her."

"What? What are you talking about? I never even talked to you."

"You love her," he said. "I know you love her. You're just in denial."

"I don't even know why you would do this or why you would say this? That's a lie."

But Rose and Norbert just kept saying the same thing. "We've all been there…we've all struggled with our identity."

I couldn't believe this was happening. No one had ever thought I was gay. Yes, I had dealt with sexual demons and different things, but *never* had this particular issue. But that's how the enemy works—he will come in and try to confuse your mind. The assassin had used a little summer job to attack me this way. He had used Norbert and Rose because the two of them seemed to already be bound by these homosexual spirits. However, as the scripture says in Proverbs 14:12, *There is a way that seems right to a man. But its end is the way of death.*

What Rose and Norbert were saying left me angry. And at the time, I wasn't walking in my salvation, so I used some choice words with the two of them, cussing them out, which wasn't something I'd ever done.

My roommate just laughed as she listened to me and when I hung up, she made a joke out of it. "Are you sure you're not like that?" She was kidding, but I wasn't amused with her or Norbert or Rose. It was as if no matter what I did, the assassin was going to make sure he was right there with me.

My sophomore year in college didn't get much better for me. I continued to struggle academically in New Orleans and I still couldn't understand why. But when I returned home after the first semester for Christmas break, everything changed.

One night, I had been out and I decided to go visit my grandmother. When I got there, she told me, "An ambulance just took your mother to the hospital."

"What?" I said.

She nodded. "She just left."

When she said that, I wondered if the ambulance I'd just passed had been taking my mother to the hospital.

My grandmother said, "You need to go to the hospital to check on her."

"What happened?"

"Your mom and I were fussing and she fell in the kitchen."

"That's why she's going to the hospital?" I asked, not sure why a little fall would make her need medical care.

"Well, she said she couldn't get up. She couldn't move."

"Okay, let's get right over there."

When I turned to my grandmother, she said, "I'm not going. You can go and see about her."

I didn't have time to ask my grandmother what that was about. I just hopped in my car and as soon as I started driving, I prayed. Inside, I asked myself a whole lot of questions: what did my grandmother mean when she said my mother couldn't get up? Did that mean she couldn't move? What was wrong with her?

I had lots of questions and I didn't know what to think. My mother was so strong, but this news had me more than worried… I was afraid.

"Please God," I prayed over and over. "Let my mom be okay."

At the hospital, I jumped out of my car and when I rushed inside, I discovered that my mom was in the Emergency Room. The attendant and the nurses allowed me to go back to where they had my mother resting and when I found her, she was crying profusely.

"Mom?" When I called out to her and she looked up, her sobs became louder.

"Kayle," she cried, "you have to tell Mom that I'm so sorry. Tell her that I'm so sorry and that I didn't mean it."

On the ride to the hospital, all I'd been thinking about was that my mom would be okay. I hadn't thought about what happened between her and my grandmother. As my mother cried, I tried to calm her down, telling her it was okay. "Don't worry about it, I'll tell her. Let's just make sure that you're okay."

She finally calmed down and I was able to stay with my mother until she was admitted into the hospital. Then, the doctor came back with a diagnosis.

"Your mother had a stroke."

"A stroke?" I was beyond shocked. My mom was young; how had she had a stroke?

"Yes. We're going to run some tests to see why this happened."

It took two days for the doctors to perform all the tests and come back to me with the devastating news.

"Your mom has a brain tumor."

"Brain tumor?" I felt like I couldn't breathe.

"Yes. A very large brain tumor and there are several smaller ones in the back of her head. We're going to have to take her into surgery in the next couple of days."

The doctor explained they were going to remove the large tumor because it was pressing against her skull. The others, they were going to leave alone.

Once I had that conversation with the doctor, I made the decision—I was not going back to New Orleans. There was no way I would be able to return to school knowing my mother was at home sick. All I wanted to do was help her through her illness. I'd take care of the house; I'd take care of Gayle. I didn't want her to have to worry about anything except getting well.

Stepping up was nothing new for me. I'd been raised to function as an adult at all times.

A few days later, my mom went into surgery. It was so hard waiting for those hours that she was in the operating room. But then things got worse. When my mother came out of surgery, I thought I could leave the hospital just for a few hours to check on Gayle, get something to eat, and then, I'd come back. I wasn't gone long—but it was long enough for my mother to slip into a coma.

The thought of brain surgery had been scary enough and now this? However, what was scarier was how my mother acted while she was in a coma. She was unconscious and wasn't supposed to be responding to anything, but all of a sudden, my mother would scream my name. "Kayle," she would yell. "Make Kayle do it. Just make Kayle do it."

My mother was literally in a coma, yet she was speaking… about me! I had no idea what she was talking about.

The first time it happened, I rushed over to her bed. "Mom. What is it?"

Her eyes were closed and I could tell she couldn't hear me. Of course, she couldn't hear me…she was in a coma! That didn't stop her from screaming, though. She just kept screaming my name. There was nothing I could do to make her stop and I felt helpless. I broke down in tears.

I felt like I was in a mental whirlwind, there were so many thoughts swirling through my mind and the major one was that my mother had a brain tumor, and was now in a coma. I was so afraid that I was going to lose her.

I began to pray to God, telling Him, "Please, Lord, you cannot take my mother. You cannot take her from me and Gayle."

My mother and I had just gotten to the point where we had a real relationship. We talked to each other as adults, I enjoyed being with her and now, I was afraid that would all end. I prayed and prayed and prayed so hard to God not to take that away.

I had asked my great aunt, who was like a spiritual mother to me to come and pray for my mother. The day she arrived at the hospital, she'd brought another lady with her.

They walked into the room while my mother was screaming my name and I was leaning over her, asking her what did she want me to do? When my aunt called out to me, I turned and hugged her, relieved that there was someone else there with me. She held me, trying to calm my tears.

Then, she introduced me to Apostle Janice Dillard. When Apostle Dillard looked at me, I saw the concern in her eyes. "Baby," she said, "why are you standing here listening to this? Why don't you go home until the nurses can get your mom settled?"

I hadn't thought about leaving my mother, but I did need a little break. With my mom screaming like that, I couldn't stop crying. So while my aunt and the Apostle stayed there, I left so that I could get some fresh air and breathe for a moment. I went home and slept.

When I returned the next morning, my mother had settled down. The Apostle had been right...and Apostle Janice Dillard has been in my life ever since.

About a week later, my mother came out of the coma and after being in the hospital for a little less than a month, she was finally released to come home. I was going to be the primary caregiver for my mother, but one of my aunts, who was a nurse, came to our house to help me whenever she could. My mother had come home in a wheelchair, but she was determined that, with physical therapy, she wouldn't be in the wheelchair for that long.

Those weren't just words. My mother put in the work to get physically better and we were all praying for her. In just two months, God took my mother from a wheelchair to a walker to a cane. It was incredible to watch her transformation. It was as if with each step, God was raising my mother up.

Each day my mother seemed to be getting better, so much so that I was finally able to get a job. I took a position at Burdines so that I could get out a little and would have something more to do. I also wanted to help out financially. Even though my mother wasn't one hundred percent well, we continued to build our relationship and were getting closer—and that had been my prayer. I'd prayed and access was granted.

It was a joy for me to take care of my mother and for us to get closer.

But then just about a month after my mother had come home, we received devastating news. Somehow, my mother had contracted HIV. This was in the early 90's and no one knew a lot about the illness, except that it was deadly. The doctors were never able to determine for sure how my mother contracted the virus, but finding out about this left us all in a state of despair, especially since the doctor couldn't give us any kind of prognosis. Like I said, at that time there was so little known about the virus that caused AIDS and the doctors were still concerned about the tumors that remained on my mother's brain. I knew God to be a healer, so my question was why had he not fully healed my mom?

My mother had made her way back from a stroke and a coma and paralysis, and now just a few months later she had to face this? I couldn't believe this was happening to her.

This news was mentally draining and devastating. But once again, I stepped up. I had to be the adult in the house, I had no other choice. There was something else where I had no choice—I had to start seeking God in a different way. I began to talk to Him a lot more and one thing about my relationship with God was that I didn't fear questioning Him. "Why, God?" was what I asked Him all the time. I asked God to explain to me all that was going on in my life. Why was this happening to my mother? Why was all of this happening to me?

Each day the weight felt heavier and heavier on my shoulders. We were fine financially because of the money my mom had coming in from the school board where she'd worked. So, it got to the point where I wanted to quit my job because it was so much taking care of my mom and my sister at the same time.

However, my mom never wanted me to do that. "I'm going to be okay, Kayle," she kept telling me. "You need to keep your job so that you can take care of yourself and buy the things that you want."

I knew my mother didn't want me to leave my job because she didn't want to wear me out; she didn't want to do that to her child.

It was hard, but I did as my mother asked and I kept my job. I spent the time in my car, driving back and forth to work, crying out to the Lord, praying that He would hear me and He would heal my mother.

Every day I pressed on. I had no other choice, I had to. My mother pressed on, too, and during this time, she mended her relationship with my grandmother. I never knew what had happened between the two of them the night my mother collapsed at my grandmother's house, but it didn't matter. They were back together and often while I was at work, my mother would visit my grandmother. It was a great way for her to get out of the house and the time they spent together was good for both of them.

For a few weeks, life seemed to settle down. While my mother was still ill, it seemed as if she was getting better. She was able to function a great deal on her own. Then one day when she was out at my grandmother's house, she slipped in the bathroom and hit her head on the side where a bone plate hadn't been placed. Once again, my mother had to be rushed to the hospital.

This time, she wasn't admitted, but that fall caused my mother to regress. Again, her brain began to swell and from that point, she was in and out of the doctor's office, then in and out of the hospital. After so many doctor's appointments, one day, the doctor told my mother and me, "I'm so sorry; there's nothing else I can do."

Just four months after my mother had her stroke, she was released to hospice care and we felt nothing but despair. Those words from the doctor took away her hope and we went into a downward spiral.

When I wasn't in my mother's presence, I spent all of my time crying out to God. I didn't want my mom to hear my anguish and desperation, but when I was alone, I would close my eyes, bow my head and ask Him the same thing over and over. "Lord, what was going on? She's Your child, Lord. My mother is a Christian, she gave her life to You. So why would You allow this to happen to her? Why would You allow her to suffer this way?" Then, I told God something that surprised me. "I would rather for You to take her than to have her suffer this way."

That day when I opened my eyes from my prayer and looked up, I saw a vision of myself in a black dress, wearing a hat. The thing was—I didn't even wear hats.

That was when I knew...it was only a matter of time.

# CHAPTER 8

The days were long and hard. At least my mother was in hospice at home. If she experienced any kind of pain or distress, someone was always there with her. But for the most part, I took care of my mother myself.

This time became so difficult for her. She wasn't sleeping and she sweated profusely, which was something I didn't understand at the time, although now I know is one of the first signs of impending death. I cared for my mother the best that I could, using a huge towel to wipe the sweat from her body, trying to keep her as comfortable as possible, and praying, praying, praying over her all the time. I didn't know all the stages of death, but I could see it coming. I knew my mother was dying.

After several nights of my mother suffering this way, one morning, I called my aunt who'd been helping me and told her my mother hadn't had a good night. "She was sweating even more than usual," I said. "She doesn't look good; I think I should call nine-one-one."

"Okay," my aunt said. "I'll be right over and we'll go to the hospital together." After I hung up, I sat with my mother. I knew she was just holding on.

When my aunt arrived at our home, she hugged me, tried to tell me that everything would be fine and then she said, "Go take a shower, and then we'll go to the hospital."

"Okay," I said. My plan was to get into the shower and then get right out so we could take care of my mother quickly. But almost as soon as that water hit me, I broke down. I couldn't do anything else but pray. As I stood there praying under the shower's water, I heard music. It took me a moment to recognize that old Negro spiritual: *We are Climbing Jacob's Ladder.*

The more I cried, the more I prayed, the louder the song rang in my ears. I felt as if there were angels in that bathroom with me as I cried and I prayed and I listened to the song.

Then, I heard a scream, a sound I'd never heard before. I jumped out of the shower, wrapped myself in a towel and dashed to my mother's room. Just for a second, I stared at my mother and my aunt…and then, I passed out right there.

Here I was, only twenty one years old, but I was grateful that my mother had raised me the way she did. I was way more mature than my age and because of that, I was able to handle all of her funeral arrangements.

On the day of my mother's funeral, I was so mentally exhausted and so emotionally messed up, that the little strength I had left in me I could only use for my sister. Any energy that was in me came from my sister. I knew I had to be strong and I had to keep going for her. I looked at it this way—if I broke down, who was going to take care of my sister?

The whole time I was moving through this process, I remembered what my mom had told me: "*Kayle, I'm going to give you this baby. This baby is yours.*"

Her words echoed in my mind every time I looked at Gayle and that kept me going. I accepted that I now had a ten-year-old who was my responsibility. So as far as I was concerned, I had one job—and that was to make sure that my sister and I were all right.

Once we buried my mother, there were a few changes that I knew I needed to make and the primary one was that I needed to rededicate my life to God, especially since I had strayed away from Him while I was in college. It wasn't that I was doing anything all that bad. I wasn't running in the streets, I wasn't in drugs, I wasn't hanging out with the wrong crowd. But Marc and I had been sexually active and God just wasn't at the center of my life anymore. I hadn't even been going to church regularly and that didn't bother me.

It had been an interesting time because as I was straying, my mother's relationship with God was getting stronger. Not only had she been going to church, but she strengthened her faith by reading and watching evangelists on television for hours. She studied and really wanted me to get back to the Lord, too. But at the time, I'd been thinking that I just wanted to live my life the way I wanted.

The death of my mom changed my thinking. There was a lot on me now and the only way I'd be able to make it was with the Lord in the center of my life. I was able to press on because as 2 Corinthians 5:8 says, *To be absent from the body and to be at home with the Lord.* So, I knew that my mother had made her life right with God. She was at home with Him, and now it was time for me to be at home with Him here on earth once again.

# CHAPTER 9

One thing about the enemy is that he knows how to trick you. He will always send someone into your life who you

will like, but who may not be for your good.

When I met Marc in high school, like I said before, I immediately liked him. He was a gentle soul, very loving, caring and understanding. My mother liked him, too, but there was one thing she knew. She always quoted Mark 3:25 to me, *If a house is divided against itself, that house will not be able to stand.*

My mother said that because Marc was of a different religion. He was part of a religion called IDMR—the acronym stands for: Institute of Divine Metaphysical Research and he was very active, participating in their weekly meetings just as I was becoming stronger in my faith.

That didn't matter to me, though. I loved Marc and he loved me, so I didn't listen to her. Marc and I got married just six months after my mother passed away in October 1992.

Our marriage sent our families into a frenzy—neither one of our families wanted us together because of our different religious beliefs. Looking back, I know for sure this was just another assignment of the assassin, but of course, I didn't know that at the time.

In the beginning, our marriage was beautiful. Marc was a wonderful husband because he was a wonderful man. Later, he would become just as great a father. Truly, he was the best man that *I* could have ever chosen.

When Marc and I first got married, we stayed in the house where I'd lived with my mother; it seemed like the best thing that we could do, especially since Gayle was comfortable there, too. So Marc moved in and we began our life together.

Now that I didn't have to take care of my mom, I had to make decisions about my life. There was no way that I could (or even wanted to) go back to college, but I wanted to do something with my life. I decided to do what my mother had encouraged me to do—I decided to go to school to become a cosmetologist. Marc was very supportive of the idea.

Once I got inside that classroom, I felt like I was home. It seemed like my mom had been right all along. She always said I had a gift and as I sat in those classes, it felt that way, too. I felt comfortable, it felt natural. I was just adding on to what my mom had already taught me.

After a year, I graduated and received my license before I started my first job in a beauty salon. Now, I'd always known that God had anointed me to be an entrepreneur and I would have my own business. However, first, I wanted to gain experience and I worked with a woman who was an extremely talented cosmetologist. I wasn't there long before I began thinking and planning to get my own business.

Things had been so good and so quiet for a while after my mother passed away, that I had almost forgotten about the assassin. So this time, when the enemy came for me, I wasn't ready; I didn't see him coming.

One day, I left the beauty shop where I'd been working to get some more supplies. The errand was supposed to be quick, but as I rushed out of the beauty supply store, I was stopped by a man.

He was professionally dressed and polite, when he approached me. "Excuse me, ma'am," he said. "This may sound like a strange request, but I'm trying to give some money to the local church here and I was wondering if you'd be able to help me."

I heard church…he wanted to give money…he needed my help. Of course, I would help him. I was so in love with God, anything I could do for one of his people, I would do.

He gave me the name of the church, but I'd never heard of that church before. As we talked, another man, a friend who was with him, joined in the conversation.

We talked about the church for a little while before the first guy asked me if I could give him a ride. To this day, I cannot tell you how he ended up in the car with me with his friend in his car following behind us. I'm not sure why I was so gullible, and I can't remember what I was thinking at the time. I think it was because he kept talking about this church and how much he wanted to help this church financially. Those words blinded me to everything else. I wanted to do anything I could for someone who had a love for God.

Anyway, I agreed and when we got in the car, our conversation about God and the church continued. Then, when the guy said, "You know what I was thinking. It might be better if you give the church the money. I can just give it to you."

Now, this might have been the point when most people walked away, but I was ignorant to the enemy's devices. I never expected the enemy to come at me talking about God. So I listened as he went on to explain that he had about $10,000 and he would leave that money with me; he would just need me to give him some money in exchange.

Looking back, it seems as if I was really naïve, and I was at the time because after talking to him, we ended up at my bank where I withdrew $6,000. The only reason I had that much money in my account was because of my mother; this was money that she had left to me.

However, it didn't seem to be a problem. In fact, this was going to work out in my favor. He was going to give me $10,000. I'd give the church the $6,000 that I was giving to him and I'd keep the difference.

I withdrew the money and outside of the bank, I once again agreed to give the church $6,000 and we exchanged money.

"Thank you so much," he said.

"You're welcome," I told him. "I'm glad I was able to help."

Then, he jumped back into the other car with his friend and they sped away.

I got into my car and drove straight to my grandmother's house. I wanted to talk to her about the church because I wanted to get this money to them right away. She knew so many people in the Christian community and I was sure that she would not only know this church, but she would know the best way for me to get this money to them.

When I got to my grandmother's house, I explained to her what happened with the men at the beauty supply store. "Here's the money he gave me," I said innocently.

I opened up the package and my heart sank all the way to my feet. There were a couple of ones on the outside, but on the inside, there was nothing but a bunch of newspapers cut up to look like dollar bills. I was stunned, shocked and so hurt. I fell to the floor and cried. How could God let this happen to me when all I was trying to do was help His people?

I felt complete devastation; this was my mother's money that she'd left for me and Gayle. When I met that man, my mind was so far away from the enemy. I thought I was talking to an angel, but that was my first experience with entertaining angels unaware. Yes, I was talking to an angel—an angel of darkness that the Word of God warns about in Matthew 7:15: *Beware of false prophets, who come to you in sheep's clothing, but inwardly are ravenous wolves.*

Finally, my grandmother made me get up from the floor and I called the police. It didn't take long for them to get there and as the two officers listened to my story, I could tell right away, they felt sorry for me.

When I finished, one of the officers said, "I'm sorry, ma'am, but you've been flimflammed." They let me know there was probably no way I'd be able to get the money back. "Most of the time," the officer continued, "we never catch these types of criminals."

Once the police left, I just sat there and cried and questioned God. "Why would you allow this to happen to me?" I asked Him. "Why would you allow your child to be robbed this way? Why God?"

When I left my grandmother's house a few hours later, I was still sobbing. I jumped into my car and sped home. All I wanted to do was get into my bed. Marc asked me what was going on and of course, I told him. But even he couldn't console me. I just stayed in bed and cried.

Two days later, while Marc was at work and Gayle was at school, my best friend, Gwen, came over. I only got out of the bed long enough to answer the door. She followed me back into my bedroom and after I crawled back into bed, I told her everything that happened.

After she heard the whole story, Gwen said, "It's all right. It's all right. This stuff is going to pass over."

But nothing she said calmed me. Nothing calmed me until I heard God's voice: *This doesn't even compare to the blessings that I have for you.*

That was when I finally stopped crying—when I heard the voice of God.

God gave me peace that night, but still, this was another example of the assassin coming in, attacking me, but I was too spiritually blind to be able to see.

Still, even though I struggled in this spiritual battle with the assassin, God remained on His Daddy duty. He came to me to let me know that yes, this had happened, but that He had something much greater.

*"You're getting ready to walk into a greater zone,"* God told me. *"It's hard for you to see because you're not there yet. But once you come into the full knowledge of who you are and who you belong to, you will know that the wealth of the wicked has been laid up for the righteous. You will know that now you are the head; you will never be the tail. But I have to get you to that point."*

I still had not come into the full knowledge of understanding the power of God. My faith was there, but I didn't have the knowledge. Romans 10:17 says, *So faith comes from hearing, and hearing by the Word of Christ.*

My faith had to continue to build. I was young in my Christian walk, but God had His hands on me. I was still stumbling, still falling, still having valley experiences and still walking through landmines. I was able to keep walking, though, because God was there. I was able to keep on because God said He would allow me to go through these things, but He always had me.

There would be many more battles to come, there would be times when I didn't understand, but I had to go through some things. That was just the way it was when you were walking with Christ.

It was because I had to go through these things that God sent Destiny Helpers into my life to help me, guide me, and keep me. Throughout my life people would step in during times when I was in situations where I could have easily been dead. There were so many times when Satan had the opportunity to kill me.

But whenever the enemy came after me that way, God would send a Destiny Helper. It was His way of letting me know that He was there. He wanted me to know who He was. He wanted me to know where I got the strength to make it through each situation, so that I would never think I'd come through by my own might or power. With every situation, God wanted me to know that I'd reached the other side because of Him.

Like Romans 3:4 says, *Let God be true, but every man be a liar.*

Once I heard God's voice, I was able to let that situation with that man scamming me go and once again get focused. I returned to work at the salon, but the desire of my heart was to still have my own place. One night, while I was at a prayer meeting at my grandmother's house, I prayed to God about opening my own salon and at the end of the meeting, my cousin, Verdie Mae Wilkes, who always spoke into my life said to me, "You're looking for a beauty salon. And it's on the corner of Atlantic and 31st, right here in Pompano. There is someone working there right now; another lady owns the space, but she's going to sell that salon to you. And the hands of God are going to be so heavily upon your business, there won't be room for anybody to sit. Your blessings will be in that salon, so when you get a chance, go over and talk to her about purchasing the salon."

Because I knew of the power of prophecy in my cousin's life, I immediately jumped on what she told me to do. I did my research and realized I had a friend who knew the owner. My friend reached out and just like the prophetess told me, the woman was ready to sell her business.

It didn't take much more for us to make the deal happen. After a couple of meetings, I was able to buy it and now I was the owner of a salon. Because I knew God was in the middle of this, I asked the Lord what the name of my business should be. He told me clearly to name my business: Dare II Be Different.

The name of my salon was birthed off of a prophetic word. Now, I was ready to go. The first thing I did was talk to my best friend, Gwen. She and I had promised each other that we'd open a business together when we were in cosmetology school together. She was going to take care of the manicures/pedicures while I focused on hair.

It didn't take us long to open the business since the salon was already in place. It also didn't take long for me to see that just like the prophetess said, there was an open heaven over my side of the business. The salon flourished and there was hardly room for new customers to come in. However on the other hand, Gwen struggled and over time, that became a problem between us. Ultimately, our partnership didn't work out because I ended up doing so well.

I was sad that our partnership ended that way, but what I came to understand was that when a prophetic word was spoken over your life or when God produced an open heaven over you, that didn't mean that other people were covered by that, especially if it wasn't their time or wasn't their season. We can try to pull someone in, but if it's not their time, we may be pulling them into their demise.

The prophecy for success had been spoken over *me* and not my girlfriend. So when I prospered, that was an easy place for the enemy to step in and destroy our friendship. The assassin, who had followed me even to my destiny, came in immediately. That's why the Word of God in Matthew 10:16 says, *Behold, I send you out as sheep in the midst of wolves; so be shrewd as serpents and innocent as doves.* God wants us to be as shrewd and as wise as serpents. We cannot go into situations blindly when we know there's a hit on our lives.

My partnership with Gwen ended, but even then, the good-

ness of God hovered over me and my business. The blessings were pouring out so fast that I felt as if God was blessing me as an adult for the blessings I didn't feel I had as a child.

The blessings weren't about me alone. God allowed my salon to be a place where others were trained and encouraged. It may have been a salon, but it felt like a ministry the way I was given the opportunity to talk to hundreds of people. I wanted every customer to walk out feeling as if they'd had a wonderful experience at Dare II Be Different.

# CHAPTER 10

Marc and I had been comfortable in the home where I'd lived with my mother, but then, I began to have spiritual encounters in the house. One day, it came to a head when Renda, a good friend of mine, came by early one morning. She was shaking when I opened the door for her and let her inside.

"Kayle, I have to talk to you," she said as she stepped into the living room.

"Okay," I said, cautiously. Clearly something was wrong. "What's going on?" I asked my friend.

"I talked to your mother last night." Her words shocked me, and then, she began to tell me all the things my mother had told her. As we stood there with Renda speaking and me listening, I began to feel like we weren't alone and Renda felt it, too. Someone was there with us. Was it my mother?

Renda continued telling me what happened. "I've never seen your mom before, but the reason I knew it was her was because she looked just like you. And when I was talking to her and told her that, she smiled and said yes."

"Was that all she said?" I asked.

Renda shook her head. "She told me to take care of you, to take care of her baby. She asked me to look after you for her."

When Renda said that, the presence of that spirit in the room was so strong that it gave us goosebumps and brought tears to our eyes. We were engulfed in that presence.

From that moment, I knew I was going to be all right. God was showing me that there was something greater than the first heaven, which is the earth realm.

Even though the encounter with Renda and my mom was positive and didn't take place in my house, I still believed it was time for us to move on. We'd stayed in the house for three years and now, Marc and I decided to leave the city. The four of us: Marc, Gayle, Markale (our son, whom I'll discuss later), and I moved to Coconut Creek, Florida. My mother had left us enough money so we were stable and didn't have to worry about finances the way many young couples did, and that was a blessing for us. Of course we both continued to work: me at the salon and Marc at Continental Cable, where he'd worked for many years.

Marc and I were doing well, personally and professionally. However, our marriage had me in a mental and spiritual battle. The older we became, the more Marc and I gravitated toward our own spiritual beliefs. I had wholeheartedly given Christ my life, while Marc had wholeheartedly given his life to Yeshua. That meant that we were growing in different ways. While the roots of our marriage were solid, our branches of spirituality were venturing out in opposite directions. The foundation of our marriage seemed good, but we were producing different fruit. There was never a way for us to have a complete understanding of each other. The only thing that kept us grounded in our marriage was that we truly loved each other.

However the challenges of being unequally yoked continued, especially once our children were born. Sometimes, I'd take the children to church with me, and other times, he'd take them to class with him. I felt horrible; our kids were being stretched in opposite directions and divided in two different ways.

All I can say is thank God for the prayers of the righteous because my grandmother prayed not only over me, but over my children. She prayed that my children wouldn't be lost in Marc's religion.

As time passed, Marc began going to his religious classes twice a week and on Sundays. He continued advancing in his position in IDMR and because of that, he began to put pressure on me.

"Kayle," he'd say, "I need to have a woman by my side. I need to have my wife with me when I go to class. You're going to have to convert."

My answer was always the same. "I'm not converting, Marc." I never wavered in that.

He'd shake his head. "Then I don't know how we can stay married."

Those were not words that I wanted to hear, but there was nothing Marc could say or do to convince me to walk away from Christ. I was saved, sanctified and filled with the Holy Ghost. I had rededicated my life to the Lord and I wasn't leaving God and what I knew to be true.

As Marc was growing in his faith, so was I. I had become more spiritually awakened and could really hear and know God's voice. I had come to know for myself that God had a destiny for me and with this knowledge, I was in the mode of seeking and searching Him all the time.

I was in church every Sunday, worshipping the Lord, but on one particular Sunday, things changed. I was at my grandmother's church the way I always was and as I sat in the pew, my attention was drawn to the leaders of the church in the pulpit. My eyes stayed on them and as I stared, their faces began to change—their faces became elongated, at first. Their features continued to twist and turn until I was staring into the faces of monsters. I didn't understand it; all I knew was that the four faces in front of me were ghastly.

I blinked a few times, thinking their faces would change back. However that didn't happen; what I was seeing was real. I jumped out of my seat, stepped over the other people in the pews and rushed out of the church without saying anything to anybody. I pushed open the front door and didn't even pause when I stepped into the pouring rain. That didn't matter to me, though. I had to get away.

As I scurried to my car, I heard a voice calling out behind me. "Where are you going?" the minister asked. "You can't leave now."

"I can't stay," I told him, shouting over my shoulder. "I have to go."

"But look at the sign," he insisted. "We are preparing for the next generation. Things are going to change here."

"I can't stay here," was what I kept telling him until I got into my car and slammed the door. I sped out of the parking lot as if I was running from someone.

I felt relieved when I was away from the street, but when the next Sunday came, I didn't have a church home. I didn't have any place to go. That was when my search for where God wanted me to be began.

There was no way that I was going to find my new church home on my own. I prayed to God, asking Him to lead me and finally the Lord said: *I want you to go to Revival Faith Center and watch.*

I knew about Revival Faith Center. My grandmother's sister and one of my aunts attended that church and it was led by Apostle Janice Dillard, the woman who had come to the hospital with my aunt to pray for my mother when she was in a coma.

Like the Lord told me to do, the next Sunday I went to Revival Faith Center and just sat there; I just watched.

I wasn't sure what God meant by that, wanting me to just watch. I didn't know what I was watching for, but I followed His instructions. I watched and I was still focused only on being obedient to the voice of God.

For the next three years, I attended services at that church just about every Sunday, even sometimes bringing my children there with me. I attended every event as if I were a member, even the church's revival.

I was sitting in the sanctuary, listening to the revival guest speaker, Apostle Cassie Sorrells-Brown, when she stopped all of a sudden and stared out into the congregation.

"Stand up!" she demanded.

The women in front of me glanced around and I did, too. "Stand up," she said again.

It took me a moment to realize she was talking to me. Finally, I said, "Me?"

She nodded. "Stand up!"

I was surprised she had called me out this way even though I was used to prophecy with all the prophets and prophetesses in my family. Not only that, no matter where I went, I seemed to be a magnet for prophets.

When I stood, Apostle Sorrells-Brown shouted, "There is an angel behind you! And I want to tell you this—God said, never apologize because He chose you. You should never apologize because the enemy has made somebody upset."

I just stood there and she continued.

"Your light is upsetting them," she preached and again she repeated that I wasn't to ever apologize.

When I sat back down, I'm telling you, that prophecy shifted something in my mind. It was like I became filled with wisdom.

Now I understood why I had so many trials and why sometimes, I faced a brick wall. With her prophecy, I came to understand why so many people hated on me. I used to believe people just didn't like me, but it wasn't me—it was the God that people saw in me. Darkness always despised the light. I was that ray of light that entered a room and destroyed the plans of darkness because now, the spirit of God was there.

That was just one of the times when, as I sat under Apostle Dillard's ministry, my eyes began to open. Not only was I learning about who I was in God, but He showed me the spirit realm and spiritual warfare. I was introduced to not only the kingdom of light, but the kingdom of darkness as well. I began to understand that all of the hurt that I still carried from my childhood was not going to stop me from achieving all that God had planned for me.

God wanted me to be the head and never the tail. He wanted me to be above and never beneath. His desire was for me to be the lender and never the borrower. This was the message I was getting sitting under the spiritual tutelage of Apostle Janice Dillard. She helped me to understand my life, the good and the bad.

I watched as Apostle Dillard prayed for people and I saw demons being cast out of others. I began to *understand* the scripture, Ephesians 6:12. Before I sat under Apostle Dillard,

I'd only known the words: *For our struggle is not against flesh and blood, but against the rulers, against the authorities, against the power of this dark world and against the spiritual forces of evil in the heavenly realm.*

I was in amazement at the way this great woman of God moved spiritually and was mesmerized with her anointing. Her incredible faith drew me in and I began to see and understand deliverance.

Under her, I learned who God really was. She became my Destiny Helper, the spiritual leader who would guide me to my destiny. Eventually, about two years later, I was led by God and joined her ministry. From that point forward, because of Apostle Dillard, so much of my life changed.

Once I found a church home, everything seemed to be well. I felt grounded spiritually, my business was thriving and at home, life was good—except for the spiritual part, which continued to be a huge challenge. Marc and my spiritual separation continued to widen. He continued to pressure me to leave my faith and follow him. That was his greatest desire, but that was never going to happen.

Still we stayed together, trying to make our marriage work. It came time for my sister to go off to college and we were excited to see Gayle go on to achieve great things. The change that was happening in my sister's life made me desire a change in mine as well.

One day, one of my girlfriends, Ann, came into the salon and started asking my employees, "Does anyone know of anybody who'd like to become a firefighter?" She went on to tell all of us that the city was looking for black female firefighters, specifically.

Ann hadn't been talking to me, but I said to her, "You know what? Now that Gayle is going off to college, I want to do something different. I was thinking about going back to school."

"Really?" Ann was surprised and so was everyone else. None of them could imagine me doing anything else since my business was doing so well. However, it wasn't that alone. Looking at me, none of the women could fathom me going from a full weave, make-up and always being dressed, to wearing boots and firefighter gear.

What I explained to the women was that even with my business doing well, I wanted to do something to secure my retirement.

Being a firefighter wasn't something that I'd desired, but after talking to Ann and thinking about it some more, I thought this would be a good time for me to do it. It would be different and challenging and the more I thought about it, the more excited I became.

As excited as I was about that idea, my family's reaction was the opposite. When I told one of my great-aunts that I was going to become a firefighter, she glared at me and said, "The devil is a liar!"

Everyone in my family had the same reaction. No one could figure out why I would even consider this. It wasn't like I had a history of firefighters in my family. I didn't know anyone who was a firefighter.

Their advice was all the same. "Don't do it."

Even Marc, who had always been supportive of my career moves, wasn't sure about this. "You know, Kayle, I tried that when I was younger and, it's really hard," he said. "I seriously doubt you'll be able to do it." He shook his head. "I just can't see you doing it."

"Oh, are you saying I can't do it?" I asked Marc.

He shook his head. "You can't do it."

That was all I needed to hear. "Watch me," I told him because I'd always been the type of person that if someone told me there was something I couldn't do, that little wheel in my head started spinning trying to figure out how to do it. Plus, while I understood the dangers, I also knew I would be protected; anything that I wanted to do and asked God for, He would give it to me and keep me safe. I was walking in Proverbs 3:6: *In all your ways acknowledge Him and He will make your paths straight.*

While everyone was still telling me no, I began seeking out men who knew something about the fire department. My brother's best friend was a firefighter and I talked to him. He gave me the information I needed, telling me what my next steps should be. I signed up immediately for the EMT classes.

What I didn't know at the time was that while I was going into a field of physical fire, I was putting myself in the path of a spiritual fire, one that would be all-consuming. By becoming a firefighter, I was going to become even more spiritually challenged, and that would lead me to becoming more spiritually awakened.

When I began my EMT classes, I couldn't say I had a lot of things going for me. I wasn't the classic candidate—I wasn't very athletic; I wasn't a runner or anything like that. However what I had over everyone else was my determination. Once I became determined, it was going to happen if for no other reason than my will.

One of the things I had to do as part of my preparation to be a firefighter was to go to North Broward Hospital to do my clinicals. On that day, as I sat there with the rest of my class, I found myself wrestling with the thought of becoming a firefighter. Was this something that God really wanted me to do? It was the pushback from my family that was affecting me the most.

As I sat there in the waiting room with my peers, all of a sudden, a little girl, a toddler around two years old, slid down from her mother's lap and waddled over to me. Then, she wrapped her tiny arms around my leg. She held on to my leg so tightly, as if she never planned to let me go.

When I looked down at her, she was looking up at me with her eyes filled with what I called liquid love. I reached down and embraced her.

My instructor glanced at me and said, "Is she with you?"

"No, sir. I don't even know her." I looked over at the woman who'd been with the little girl and at that moment the scripture Isaiah 43:19 came to my mind, *Behold I will do something new. Now it will spring up.* This interaction helped me to see that God had anointed me to do this as an EMT. God gave me the permissive will of my desire.

Being a firefighter wasn't what He called me to do, but it was a desire that I had in my heart. Because He loved me much, it was like God was saying: *Kayle is bringing her desire to me.* As God was rebuilding, rebirthing and restructuring me, He was going to give me what was in my heart at that time and He was going to use me to be a light inside the darkness.

Still, even after that revelation, I had to battle all the way through school. The assassin was always there, particularly when I was studying. There were times when I'd have to close down my entire life to comprehend one paragraph of what I was reading. There was so much to learn and none of it came easy, especially as the only black female. In the end, however, I achieved my goal. I made it through the school and I was now EMT-certified and firefighter-certified. God brought me through it.

Now, I was ready to be hired and once again, my friend, Renda, was there to help. She knew the Chief of the fire department and she told me to go speak with him so that I would get hired right there in Pompano Beach.

I went to Chief Bentley, who happened to be a black man, and before I had the chance to say too much to him, he gave me one of those long, up and down glances, then said, "Why would a woman like you want to come to an environment like this?"

I told him a little about myself and added, "I really want to become a firefighter and I want to work here because I grew up in this city." From my heart, I believed that I would be a greater help to the citizens of Pompano Beach because I knew them.

What I said didn't seem to matter to the Chief. After I had said all of that, he asked, "Why would a woman want to come over here and blow black smoke out of her nose?" Before I had the chance to answer him, he added, "Why would a woman like *you* want to do this? Because you do understand that they are going to come after you. It is not easy here; it is not easy doing this."

I didn't really understand where he was coming from. I didn't know whether he was trying to discourage me because I was a woman or because I was black. This was something new to me.

I told the Chief that the fact this career was hard didn't bother me. I was determined and willing to work hard.

It didn't matter what I said, though, the Chief just didn't agree. Finally he told me, "I can't do it. You don't even know what you're getting into and I won't hire you here."

"So what am I going to do?" I asked him. I was upset because he didn't have a good reason for not hiring me. He hadn't asked me anything about my skills. He was purely talking to me as a woman…a black woman.

"You'll be okay," he said. "Apply in another city."

I walked away from him feeling defeated and the moment I left his office, I began to pray. When I got home, I called Renda and told her what happened.

"I'm going to call him," she said, sounding as determined as I'd been when I'd walked into the Chief's office. "But Kayle," she began, "you need to go back in there and talk to him."

I had never been one to give up, but I knew the Chief wasn't going to change his mind. "He already said he won't hire me," I protested. "What am I supposed to say to him now?"

"Tell him to put himself in your shoes."

Renda pushed me to go back and I did. I told him about walking in my shoes and then, I repeated all the things I'd said to him before. My second visit didn't change a thing—again, the Chief said no.

I was ready to give up. I wasn't moving to another city, and if the Chief wouldn't hire me in Pompano Beach, there was no place for me to have this new career. A few days later, though, I was at the salon and the Chief called me. "I'm going to stop by your business," he said.

"Okay," I said, wondering what he wanted.

The next day, he came by and Dare II Be Different was as busy as ever. I couldn't even get to him right away when he came in because I had to handle a few things. So the Chief just stood in front of the salon and watched all the hustling and bustling that was going on.

When I was finally able to get over to the Chief, he said, "I just wanted to come by and see." After talking to me for just a little bit, he left.

His visit gave me a little bit of hope, so I called him the next day and once again, gave him my plea. "Chief," I said, "I want to work for the city of Pompano Beach so much. I can do it. I know I can."

This time, he said, "Well, come back to my office."

I couldn't get over there fast enough. When I got to his office, I was told to fill out the application, before I was led to take a polygraph test and a psychological exam. After it was all done, the Chief told me that I was going to be in his next training class.

I was thrilled. The assassin had been raging, but in the end, I was hired. No matter what obstacle the enemy had put in my way, I just kept pressing forward. The scripture says, *Submit therefore to God. But resist the devil and he will flee from you.* I had resisted and persisted and I had won!

The Chief did ask me to make one promise to him, though. He said, "You must promise me that no matter what happens, you will stay on course. You must promise me that you will make it through probation."

"I promise you," I told him, "I will not quit," I said, believing that I had already demonstrated that to him.

The moment those words left my lips, the assassin ran and made haste with the enemy. The hell doors opened from there. Once again, I was going to have to rely on James 4:7; I was going to have to resist and resist and resist the enemy time and time again in order to make him flee.

# CHAPTER 11

I was a firefighter! I'd made it when no one thought I could and I was enjoying my new career. What was great about being a firefighter was that I didn't have to give up the salon and it was still doing well. Like my cousin had prophesied, the windows of heaven hovered over that salon. The salon had not only paid for everything while I was in school to become a firefighter, but I didn't even have to worry about the everyday management of Dare II Be Different. I had rented out my salon chairs, so everyone was responsible for themselves. They were all independent contractors and that worked well for me. The business stayed successful and God remained faithful.

The first few months were great, but it didn't stay that way. It didn't take me long to realize that I was trying to become part of something that had been built on a 'good old boys' network. The atmosphere in the firehouse wasn't conducive for this young black female entrepreneur/firefighter.

I could imagine how I looked to the five guys I worked with at the station during any particular shift. However, I wasn't there to take away anything from any one of them. I didn't come in as a young black girl looking for a big career. I was there seeking something in addition to my business and even though I was only twenty-nine years old, I was looking forward and thinking about retirement.

However, it was tough to be there. Coming in, I had a one-year probationary period and all I kept thinking was that I had made the promise to the Chief—that no matter what, I was going to stay the course. But it was challenging because I was in a war. Although I felt the battle in the natural, I knew it was spiritual warfare. I knew as Ephesians 6:12 says, *For our struggle is not against flesh and blood, but against the rulers, against the powers, against the world forces of this darkness, against the spiritual forces of wickedness in the heavenly places.*

On a regular basis, I experienced racism and discrimination. Before I became a firefighter, these were things I'd heard or read about. To that point in my life I hadn't personally experienced any of this. However, now I was personally being attacked this way, verbally and psychologically.

When I walked into a room, the glares I received from the guys told me the thoughts that were on their minds: *what's she doing here...we don't want her here...she doesn't deserve this job.* This attitude wasn't coming from everyone, but there enough men who felt this way to make me feel uncomfortable.

The comments I overheard were much worse than their glares. "She reminds me of a monkey," or "She belongs in the kitchen."

Even though I knew there was a hedge of protection around me, I could still feel the darkness trying to engulf me. I wasn't going to allow it to overtake me, though. I kept showing up to work with one goal—do my job and do it well. My plan was just to go to work, work as hard as I could, then go home. I wasn't going to turn back, but I was going to need God to get through this.

When I'd been with the department for six months, I was assigned to Station 11 and a lieutenant I didn't know. Very quickly, though, I came to realize that the man I was working for was Satan himself—and the lieutenant took me through hell.

This man seemed to have one objective and that was to break me down. He didn't hide his hate, he never tried to cover up his black heart. He came after me every chance he had.

The lieutenant would single me out from the other firefighters and put me through training when there was no training going on. He would have me outside with my gear on, laddering the building, which weighed hundreds of pounds. I would be alone, doing things that I now know I wasn't supposed to be doing.

Then, he constantly attacked me with his words, telling me, "No one wants you here," and, "You're not even supposed to be here," and, "You don't belong, you don't fit in here."

I tried to walk on eggshells around him because I knew he was demonically driven. I was working at a fire station and

I was in the fire. Truly, I felt like the three Hebrew boys in the Book of Daniel. Shadrach, Meshach, and Abednego had been commanded to bow to the King and when they didn't, were tossed into the fiery furnace. I wasn't bowing, I wasn't giving in, even as the lieutenant was throwing me into the fire.

Every shift I worked for him, I cried. It got to the point where I really didn't want to do this anymore; I wanted to quit. Of course I couldn't because the Chief had warned me of this and I'd made that promise that I was going to keep.

I felt so alone because I couldn't share what was going on at the station with anyone. I certainly couldn't tell my family because they were the ones who told me not to do this. So if I told them what was going on now, their advice would have been to quit. I had to keep it in and that made it even more difficult. However, every day, I handled it. I handled the things the lieutenant said to me and the things he made me do.

All I could do was turn to God and cry out. "Why is this man doing this?" I asked the Lord. "What kind of man would do this?"

Was the lieutenant treating me this way because I was black? Was it because I was a woman? There were times when I thought about talking to another lieutenant or maybe even going to the Chief. In the end I didn't do anything. I just kept trying to fight that uphill battle.

When I thought about it, though, I realized I'd been here before. How many times had I faced this kind of adversity? This was nothing but the assassin using yet another person to get to me. I had to remember what this was—a spiritual battle. That meant that God was right by my side.

As the end of my probationary period got closer, I began to wonder what was going to happen? What was the lieutenant going to do? I knew what was *supposed* to happen: when probation was over, each of us would be given an evaluation. At that point, our pay would be increased 2%, 4% or 6%…or we could get nothing! Like I said, I didn't know which way it would go with me.

On the day my probation period ended, I was given my evaluation. I closed my eyes before I looked at the paper and then, I saw it—I had only been given 2%! I couldn't believe it. I hadn't given 100% effort, I'd given 120% every single day, not to mention all the extra work that the lieutenant had given to me.

This evaluation was unfair and I didn't want to settle for this. However, when I spoke to the lieutenant, he gave me no choice. He said to me, "If you don't sign your evaluation, you're automatically fired."

He spoke nonchalantly, as if he didn't care. I looked straight at him, knowing that he was the assassin. The evaluation wasn't fair at all, but there was no way he was going to get me to quit. So I signed the evaluation. There was nothing else I could do.

All signed evaluations were sent to the administration office, and within an hour, I received a call from one of the battalion chiefs.

He asked, "Did you see your evaluation?"

"Yes, sir."

"Well, why did you sign that?" He sounded perplexed.

"I didn't agree with it, but the lieutenant said I had to or else I'd be fired." I stopped there, not wanting to tell him all the things the lieutenant had said to me and all the things he'd done to me. It wasn't that I was trying to protect the man the assassin had used; it was that I didn't know who I could trust.

But the battalion chief pressed on, "What? He told you that?"

"Yes," I said.

"Well, you know what? You have another twelve hours that you're here, and I'll give you that time. Then, you tell me what you want to do about this."

"Yes, Chief," I said.

He went on, "Because I'm telling you right now, you don't have to accept this. You can fight it and you can win."

I could fight? The lieutenant hadn't told me that, but with what the chief was saying, I realized that once again, I was being put into the position to fight the assassin. I was being forced to fight the enemy who was trying to destroy my destiny.

I was being given a chance to call out the enemy and call Satan a liar. As John 8:44 says, *You are of your father the devil, and your will is to do your father's desires. He was a murderer from the beginning, and does not stand in the truth, because there is no truth in him. When he lies, he speaks out of his own character, for he is a liar and the father of lies.*

After thinking about it for a few hours, I called the battalion chief back. The moment he answered, I said, "You're right. I want to fight."

Just minutes after I hung up from that call, the assassin, in the form of the lieutenant, came right up to me. From the scowl on his face and his body language, I knew he'd heard that his evaluation was being challenged. When the lieutenant stood in front of me, he looked at me like he was the devil himself. "If you fight this," he said, "you're going to lose."

I knew for sure that he believed that. No one ever fought his evaluations.

He continued, "And once you lose, it's going to be worse for you." Then, as my punishment, I guess, he had me go out into the bay and spray cones for the entire night.

It didn't matter what he planned to do to me. Now that I'd been given the chance, I was going to fight. With God on my side, I knew I was going to win.

I was given a date for my hearing. At that hearing, I would go in and challenge my evaluation in front of all of the lieutenants—including the one the assassin had chosen as a weapon against me.

As I waited for the day, I had everyone in my family and Apostle Janice Dillard, who had become my spiritual mother, praying for me. I hadn't gone into the specifics of what I had been going through because I knew my family's reaction wouldn't be good. Still, I asked them to pray and they did.

On the day of the hearing, I was nervous the entire day because while I knew I was right, I didn't know what to expect.

While I was still at the station waiting to go over to the admin building, one of the other lieutenants talked to me about my upcoming hearing. "Do you know you have rights?" he asked me.

"No sir, I really don't know anything. I just know that I didn't deserve the evaluation I received."

"Well, you have rights," he said. "See that book over there?" I followed his glance to a binder on the shelves. "Open it up."

I opened the binder and right away, I figured out that this was an Evaluation Procedures Manual. I sat in the firehouse and read about the way things were supposed to be. For example, there was a training procedure that if you weren't doing something right, first, you were supposed to be told and then, you were to be given instructions and the leader was supposed to find a way to train you again. In order for a lieutenant to give you a bad mark, he had to prove that he had trained you to the best of his ability.

The entire time I'd been on probation, none of these procedures had been followed.

As I continued to read, the lieutenant said to me, "If any of these things didn't happen, you cannot be given a bad evaluation." He explained that everything in that book had to be followed.

I was so grateful to this lieutenant. He had just given me the ammunition to fight at my hearing. Still, I had one more hurdle. Now, I knew what I was going to say, but I wasn't sure how to say it. I didn't know how to talk to the men I was about to face. I didn't know their language, and once again, I turned to God. I prayed that the Lord would show up and speak through me. I prayed that these men would have hearts of flesh so that they would be able to hear me.

I arrived at the admin offices for the hearing about forty-five minutes early. I was led to the room where the hearing would be and told to wait. As I sat at the head of the table, I began to pray down the spirit of God in that place, once again asking for His assistance and His wisdom. I wanted to shift the atmosphere before the lieutenants even walked into the room.

When the men came and settled inside the room, not only was I the only woman, but I was the only African American. The spirit of fear tried to rise up in me, but I pushed it down, knowing that wasn't of God.

I sat up confidently in my chair and God planted the words on my tongue. I started with the fact that I knew what I was doing because I had been trained by each of them. I went around the room, addressing each man personally. I went back to the trainings I had with them, saying things like, "Lieutenant Brown, it had been a pleasure working with you and the way you taught me."

For about twenty minutes, I spoke, reviewing what I'd learned and reminding each man that my training with him had been stellar; I had always performed well.

Finally, I had to face the accomplice to the assassin. I said to him, "Lieutenant, the whole time working with you, you trained me on so many things. When you trained me, the reason I was sure I'd done a good job was because you never told me that I had not completed the task."

From there, I spoke to all of them as if I was the book, repeating the standard operating procedure that I'd just read. I told the lieutenant that he had never given me verbal nor written instructions that I wasn't performing any task correctly. I closed with, "And Lieutenant, if I'm doing anything incorrectly, I am a product of you. I am only doing what you taught me."

Before I left, I thanked them all for their time, for all the training I'd received in my first year and I told them that I was looking forward to a great career in Pompano Beach.

Then, I pushed back my chair, stood up and walked out of that room feeling wonderful. I felt as if there had been angels in that room with me. The assassin had come to kill me on the job, but God had brought a Destiny Helper—in the form of the lieutenant who showed me the book.

It was clear that the angels were ever-present that day, and the lieutenant's evaluation was overturned. However, that day turned out not only to be good for me, but for many who would come behind me. After my situation, the entire evaluation system changed. Evaluations would no longer be given based on opinions; evaluations would be only skill-based.

That was one of the hardest days of my careers, but it was so worthwhile and satisfying. However, just because I had that victory, that didn't mean the assassin was now going to quit. Day after day, night after night, I continued to have encounters with the enemy, but there is one night that stands out in my memory because it changed the way I behaved at the station.

All of us on the shift that night were asleep, trying to rest because we never knew when we would have to rush out on a call. The station was equipped with twin beds and I was asleep in mine when all of a sudden, I felt a cool breeze coming from under my blanket.

My eyes popped open. The room was pitch-black, so I couldn't see anything. But then, I felt the covers lift up off of me and then, hands on my feet, pulled me all the way out of the bed. I was so scared, but I didn't want to scream. There were four other guys in the room and I didn't want to wake everybody when I didn't even know what was happening. I just kept saying to myself, "Oh God, what is this?"

Once I was on my feet, I was filled with so much fear I didn't know what to do. However I didn't see anything, although I still felt the darkness.

I went into the lounge area and I sat in one of the chairs. I prayed and pled the blood of Jesus over the atmosphere, and finally, I didn't feel the demons around me anymore.

Still, I didn't go back to that room. I knew the assassin was angry because he hadn't stopped me from achieving my goal. He couldn't stop me with the evaluation, so now, he was going to use mind games.

It didn't matter what he was going to do. The enemy had to realize by now that I wasn't going to quit. Still, from that point forward, though, I only slept in one of the recliners in the lounge area. I never slept in that room again.

# CHAPTER 12

After that experience with my lieutenant, life became a bit better with me as a firefighter. There was still darkness in the station, but I was able to handle it. As I worked, Dare II Be Different continued to do well and after a while, I began to think that I was ready to take my business to the next level.

For a while, I'd been thinking about opening a day spa. I didn't have any plans; I didn't even know where I would open that business—it was just something I'd been considering.

One day, as I was transporting a patient to the hospital, I passed the Pompano Citi Centre mall. The mall was being revamped and was still under construction, but as I drove by, I felt the Lord say to me, "*What about the mall?*"

I knew He was talking about the day spa and right away, I told God, "I can't afford to put my business in there."

And the Lord said, "*Why not?*"

That was a good question. The favor of God was always on my life, even as the assassin tried to take me out, even as my husband was still trying to get me to join his religion, even with everything going on at work—I knew about God's favor. So, I started really thinking about opening a day spa at the new mall. It wasn't going to be finished for another few months, but that would give me time to do what I needed to do to prepare. I'd been operating Dare II Be Different as a sole proprietorship and so I decided to get it incorporated.

When the leasing office for the mall finally opened, on one of my days off, I dressed in a business suit, and carrying a briefcase (that didn't have anything inside of it), I went into the mall's office to speak to them about leasing one of their new retail spaces. I went in there on faith because God was the one who had led me there.

I spoke with one of the leasing managers, who told me she would be happy to draw up an agreement for me. Then, she went on to tell me everything that I'd need to be able to move into one of the mall's spaces.

"You're going to need about $69,000 to $100,000 in working capital in the bank." She explained that money would be used to build out the space and any other expenses I would have before I opened.

Even though I had no money in the bank, I smiled as if I did. Then, I filled out the applications, did all of the other paperwork and started attending the meetings the mall had for the new tenants—all without having the money that she said was needed.

Actually, I should have had that money in the bank. I'd made a lot of money over the years with Dare II Be Different, but I hadn't been a good financial steward. Still, I sat in those meetings as if I had all the money I needed to open my day spa.

The challenge was, not only didn't I have this money, but I didn't have a clue as to how I was going to get it. I knew I'd have to go to a bank, but I couldn't just walk in there and ask for money. I'd have to give them a reason to want to give me the money; I'd need a business plan.

Once again, I was back in prayer and the Lord divinely aligned me with someone to write my business plan. I wasn't surprised. Any time God was part of the plan, doors opened.

I was referred to Weilder's Business, Inc. in Hollywood, Florida, and one day, I just drove down to the company. Again, I wasn't sure how any of this was going to happen, but since God had ordered my steps, I knew this would work out.

When I arrived at the company, I was led to speak to one of the men in the office. I told him I'd heard their company did business plans.

"We do," he said, "but what I need to know is your vision. What is it that you want to do?"

That was a question that I could easily answer and from there, I began to work on Tranquility Day Spa. Once again, God gave me the name for my business, and He gave me the vision. I sat down with Weilder's and we developed my plan from all the things that God had told me. Within weeks, the business plan was completed and the first bank I submitted my plan to had given me $150,000 to start my business. I had to use my house as collateral, but this was a big deal. Now, I had the money to get started.

Once I had the money, things moved quickly. I hired an architect, who developed the plans for me to build out the physical space that I imagined. I wanted my day spa to feel like a retreat. Once I had the plans, though, I ran into the first problem. The entire buildout that I imagined was going to cost $300,000.

So, I returned to the mall management office and spoke with one of the leasing agents to explain my situation. "I have to get additional financing for my buildout."

He replied, "I know the perfect guy to help you." He gave me the information for one of his connections, a man named Bob. "Tell him I sent you and that he should help you."

I walked away from that meeting with a smile. This was just another example of a Destiny Helper stepping into my life. I called Bob and just like the agent at the mall told me, Bob agreed to help. But he said, "Tell him I'm going to do this, but he's going to owe me one."

From the moment he agreed, Bob was all in. He was an older, Jewish man who didn't know me at all, except for the referral, yet, he treated me like I was his daughter. Bob redid my paperwork, wrote letters of recommendation and was able to get me an additional $150,000 from the mall in a TI allowance. I didn't even have to pay Bob. Once again, God opened the door for a miracle and had another Destiny Helper step into my life.

Now that I had the architectural plans and the money, I hired a contractor who had been recommended by friends. The relationship with the contractor started out well, but then quickly deteriorated.

Our first challenge came because we were working on a timetable that had been given to us by the mall. I had to adhere to their schedule and there were times when I felt as if the contractor didn't care about that at all. His nonchalance about the time wasn't working for me.

Then, I was on the second floor of the mall and my plumbing had to go through the store beneath me. That turned out to be one of the worst battles. The store on the first floor was concerned about what my plumbing would do to their space. It got so bad that the contractor quit, taking a lump sum of my money with him. Now, I had to find another contractor to finish the job *and* I had to find more money.

This was a mess; I had to go to court to sue the contractor, but that was going to take a lot of time that I didn't have. Now, I was stressed. Once again, though, God stepped in with another contractor who understood my situation and who agreed to help me for very little. All I had to do was buy the materials.

Even with all of that help, this was still going to be a financial challenge. I had to get money from everywhere—from my salon, from my paychecks from the fire department. However, even with all of that, I was still going to be about $30,000 short and I didn't have a way to get that money.

The pressure continued to build and soon it became too much. One day, I went to visit my spiritual mother just to find some comfort and to pray. I cried to her, completely devastated by what had been going on and the thought that after everything, I still might not be able to make my dream come true because of the money that I needed.

My spiritual mother allowed me to vent and cry and then, she looked me straight in my eyes. "I believe in you. So how much do you need?"

I didn't even think about it when I answered her. I said, "I need $30,000 right now."

My spiritual mother didn't hesitate. She stood up, got her checkbook and wrote the check for the money I needed. When she handed it to me, I stared at the check for a moment. I hadn't come to her to ask for the money; I didn't expect her to give it to me. "I believe in you," she repeated. She knew the call God had on my life and she was my ultimate Destiny Helper. I accepted the check from her and because of her, I was able to finish and open Tranquility Day Spa.

After just a little less than a year from when I started, I opened. The spa was amazing; it was everything that I imagined. We had a huge grand opening to show everyone around the four-thousand-square-foot spa, which welcomed everyone with a twenty-foot waterfall in the lobby. The Lord had given me the vision of that structure with high ceilings and the huge waterfall that drew people in.

I had designed the spa with earth tones: gold, brown, green. From the floor to the top of the wall, everything was those colors. The fixtures were gold and white and the pedi spas were all made of glass. The space was inviting, relaxing... and so tranquil.

From the first day I opened, much like with Dare II Be Different, Tranquility Day Spa was always busy and with fifteen employees, I was able to handle it. The business was awesome. Things were a little bit tighter financially than with Dare II Be Different because the rent and the other expenses were so much more since I was in a mall. Still, it was going well.

One thing I should mention—I was the sole owner of my spa this time. The only partner I wanted was Jesus. However, while I was the owner, I didn't tell most people that. Most of the clients who came into the spa knew me as the manager and I had a very good reason for this. My experience at the fire department had opened my eyes to this world of discrimination and now that I was familiar with it, I understood that for my spa to be successful, I had to walk and operate in "their world." That meant no one could know that I owned this.

So, I operated as the manager and my business thrived. However about two years after the opening, I began to experience a bit of turbulence, something I hadn't experienced in all the years I'd had Dare II Be Different. At Tranquility Day Spa, we had been averaging about $30,000 a month in sales of products and services, which was a new level for me. I was doing well. However, it was difficult to maintain that level of the business because promises made by the mall (as to the anchor stores they were going to have to drive people there) didn't happen.

As time passed, the foot traffic in the mall never picked up and I began to struggle. Struggling in business was new for me. Dare II Be Different had the grace of an open heaven. My salon was a magnet for prosperity. However, it was different with Tranquility Day Spa. I wasn't feeling the umbrella of security and things began to tilt a bit in my business. I couldn't explain it exactly, but things weren't right; the atmosphere was shifting.

I wasn't the only one to notice the shift. One of the women who worked for me, a Brazilian lady, came to me one day. "Ms. Kayle, something's happening here."

"What do you mean?" I asked her, wanting to know because she was very spiritual.

"There's something wrong," she said. "There's something in here."

She couldn't explain it beyond the negative feelings she had and I didn't have time to stop and figure out what she was talking about specifically. I turned my attention from what she was saying and focused my efforts on just trying to keep Tranquility Day Spa afloat. I was just praying and praying and praying, telling God how I was feeling about everything that was happening. I was praying out of my emotions and fear.

What I didn't realize at the time was that God doesn't move on our emotions; God moves on faith. So my prayers were going forth without power.

Instead of standing in the middle of the salon and speaking God's word over my business, my prayers were filled with fear. I was praying, "Please, God. I don't know what I'm going to do. I don't know what to do." I was totally caught up in the emotion of the situation. I didn't remember Psalm 119:49-50 where the psalmist urges us to remind God of His promises.

While I was feeling so unsettled, the assassin came in for the kill and this time, he used my husband. While I was going through all of this emotional drama, my husband once again began to pressure me to join his religion.

"If you don't do this, Kayle," Marc said, "we'll have to get a divorce."

I wasn't surprised. The enemy was coming for me at a time when I was emotionally drained, to get me to turn my back on my Christianity. However, even in my weakened state, I wasn't going to do it.

Then one day, my Brazilian employee came to me again. "Ms. Kayle, something is going on in this place," she said with a bit more urgency than before. "Can you please pray about the spiritual things that are happening in here?"

"What's going on?" I asked her like I'd done the last time.

This time, she had more of an answer. "The other day, I was doing a facial on a client and a mirror dropped from the wall right onto her face."

That stunned me and fear gripped me immediately. I was already struggling financially. I couldn't afford something like that happening that could lead to a lawsuit.

I was walking in a posture of powerlessness. I no longer had faith in my prayers, I no longer had faith in my own oil that had been poured over me. I needed someone to pray for me because I just wasn't sure that my prayers were working anymore. Of course, I went to my spiritual mother and told her what was going on. I asked for her prayers and of course, Apostle Dillard gave them to me.

What was happening at the time, though, was that I was doing what many people do. So often we rely on our pastors (or others) to pray for us, we rely on our pastors (or others) for healing. But God told us in Acts 2:17, *And it shall be in the last days,' God says, 'That I will pour out My Spirit on all mankind; And your sons and your daughters will prophesy, And your young men will see visions, And your old men will have dreams.*

I wasn't walking in the power that God had given to *me*! The lack of faith and the filling myself with fear was destroying my promise. I was in a season of panic.

Every morning, I prayed, and then played Cindy Trimm's *The Rules of Engagement* CD. I was trying to shift the atmosphere and rid the space of any demons. However, day after day, my situation continued to worsen.

While I was in the middle of this struggle, one day a very tall white guy came into the spa. He caught my attention because he stood out. It was more than his height; he looked like somebody off of the TBN channel. He almost looked like an angel.

"I'd like to get a massage," he told my receptionist.

She set him up with one of the technicians, and after he had his massage, he paid the $100 fee. But then, he told the receptionist that he needed to speak to the owner.

She came to me and told me what he'd said. "He wants to speak to the owner."

"Was everything all right with his services?" I asked.

She nodded. "He said everything was fine, but he needed to speak to the owner. He was insistent."

I stepped out to speak to the gentleman. "Hello sir," I greeted him. I introduced myself, then asked, "How may I help you?"

"Are you the owner?"

"I'm the manager," I said. "But I really can help you. I can make sure that all of your information and concerns get to the owner. Was everything okay with your massage?"

"Yes, my massage was fine, everything was beautiful, but I must speak to the owner."

I tried to talk to him, but he wasn't going to say anything to me. "I must speak to the owner," was what he kept saying.

He left that day, but then he returned the next day and signed up for another massage. Like the day before, it seemed like he enjoyed his service, but after he paid, he once again told the receptionist that he needed to speak to the owner.

So again, she came back to get me, told me what was going on and I went back to the front to speak to this gentleman.

He greeted me with a smile and then, he asked, "Is the owner here today?"

I looked at him and said, "Yes."

"Well, I really need to speak to her. This is very important."

I realized he wasn't going to go away, so I took him aside, and we stood in front of the waterfall before I said, "Well, you're speaking to the owner."

There was shock on his face and surprise in his tone when he asked, "So you're the owner of this place?"

"Yes, sir. I'm the owner, but I like to be known as the manager."

He nodded then said, "You're a Christian?"

"Yes," I said, surprised by his question. Out of all the reasons why I thought he might want to speak to the owner, being a Christian had not made the list.

He asked, "Are you spiritual at all?"

"Yes."

"Do you know anything about demons?"

"Yes," I responded again, wondering where this was going. Then he asked, "Have you ever heard of the python spirit?"

I frowned. "No, not really."

He said, "Listen to me. There were two python spirits sent here to your business and they're coming in and out of your waterfall." We stepped away a little when he said that and then he went on to explain the characteristics of this spirit. He said that when that demon was sent to someone, it wrapped itself around the person. "I believe it's sucking the very life out of your business."

*My God,* I thought, thinking of all the things that I'd been struggling with in my business. That was exactly how I'd been feeling, as if every bit of life was being sucked out of Tranquility Day Spa.

He said, "It's going to take a team of skilled prayer warriors to come in here and pray. And it can't be you. You can't do it; you're not strong enough to do it," he said, even though he didn't know me. "A team of warriors will be able to get them out of here."

His words confirmed what had been going on, but instead of feeling relief, I felt even more fear. While I was saved, I was still spiritually ignorant about demonic forces. I was afraid because I didn't know what I was supposed to do. That's why the scripture Hosea 4:6 says, *My people are destroyed for lack of knowledge.*

As I stood there grappling with what this man had just told me, a tiny Filipino woman walked into the spa and came right up to us. The man looked at her, then turned back to me. "This is my wife," he said. "Would you mind if we prayed for you?"

For a moment, I was surprised that this was his wife, but right away, I said, "I don't mind," wanting any help I could get.

We joined hands and the three of us prayed together, right in the middle of the reception area of the spa. I noticed, though, that his prayer wasn't for the spa—he prayed for me.

His prayer was so powerful that when he finished, people came from the back of the spa asking him if he would pray for them…and he did. When he was finally able to leave, I thanked him and his wife, then ran straight back into my office. I cried as I picked up the phone and called Apostle Dillard, wanting to tell my spiritual mother everything that happened.

Once I got out the whole story, she told me to calm down and then, she spoke the word of God to me: "The devil is a lie," she said. "No weapon formed against you shall prosper and every tongue that rises up against you in judgement, you shall condemn," she added, quoting, Isaiah 54:17. She went to war for me and I needed it because the battle that I was in was even greater than I imagined.

Even after that day, though, life was still challenging at the spa. It was so hard for me to function because everything was off. The numbers were spiraling down. I was behind in rent; I was struggling to pay my employees. I was at a point of desperation. What that man had told me—that spirits were sucking the life out of Tranquility Day Spa—was happening.

I couldn't understand how this was happening, though. How could God give me something and then allow the enemy to take it away? I couldn't understand how God would allow something to be built from the ground and then allow it to be torn down. Tranquility Day Spa had been birthed by faith and I had expected the same open heaven blessings that I had with Dare II Be Different. I had expected my cup to runneth over, but my cup was not only empty, it had been sucked completely dry.

Later, I came to understand that in order for God to dress me for my destiny, I had to go through the process. I had to "go through" to "get to" what God had planned for me. Even the turmoil I experienced with Tranquility Day Spa was part of the process; it was part of God's plan.

However, as I was going through it, I didn't know that. All I knew was that I was drowning and I was so stressed, I couldn't even think. I needed to make a change and I thought that in order for me to get back to the place where I could function, I had to get away. I couldn't go too far or stay away for too long. It just so happened that I had friends who were going to Atlanta to see *The Color Purple* at that time. I decided to take the trip with them.

We traveled to Atlanta by train and that was my first time on that railway. It took us about sixteen hours to go from Florida to Georgia, but the ride didn't feel long to me. It was a soothing time, which was just what I needed. However, it wasn't restful. All kinds of thoughts still bombarded me and I didn't know what I was going to do. I was behind in my rent. I was losing employees because I couldn't afford to pay for that large staff. I felt like I was losing my grip...I felt like I was losing everything.

Still, that night in Atlanta, I enjoyed the play, but that time away wasn't enough. When I returned from the overnight trip, all of the problems that I'd left behind seemed even bigger. My biggest challenge was my rent. Even though I'd been a good tenant to this point, I was now four months behind and the mall management was not trying to be patient. They had already given me several extensions, but I also kept receiving letters—they wanted their money and if they didn't get it soon, the mall was going to close my doors on me.

I didn't have many choices. In fact, in my mind, I only had one. The night I returned to Florida, I waited until the mall was closed and then, I pulled up with two U-hauls and about five guys and emptied out my place. The next morning when the mall opened, I was gone. Handling my business that way wasn't what I wanted to do, but it was what I had to do to survive.

Just a few weeks later, I was served with legal papers. The mall sued me for a million dollars. A million dollars! I was sick; how was I supposed to handle a million dollar lawsuit? I went from lawyer to lawyer to lawyer and finally someone recommended an attorney in Coral Springs who would be able to help me.

By the time I walked into this attorney's office, I had been broken. I entered that man's office with tears in my eyes. The attorney looked up at me, told me to sit down and my story just poured out of me.

When I finished, he said, "Do yourself a favor. I'm going to charge you $1,500 to get the hell dogs off of you right now. I'm going to shift paperwork while you go and find yourself the best bankruptcy attorney ever and then, you walk away so that you and your children can live."

I left his office feeling a bit of relief and I followed his instructions. As he promised, he held the mall off until I found an attorney and declared bankruptcy. Again, this wasn't how I would have liked to handle this, but I'd been saved from the million dollar lawsuit.

Still, the assassin had come in and literally wiped me out. At this point, I had nothing. At least, there was no way that life could get worse—except it did.

A few weeks after I declared bankruptcy, I was at work at the fire station when one of the lieutenants at my station asked me if I had closed my business.

"Yes," I told him.

"And, you filed bankruptcy?"

His question surprised me, but still I said, "Yes." I wasn't trying to hide it and I guessed my bankruptcy was a matter of public record.

When he asked me what happened, I told him my story.

What I didn't know at the time was that this man sat on the board of one of the accounts, the credit union, that I had to include in my bankruptcy. After I'd shared with him what happened to me, he went back to that board and told them I had committed bankruptcy fraud. Because I had shared my story with him, I ended up being investigated for fraud. There was a chance that I would lose my job, on top of everything else that I had already lost.

In the end, it turned out that the lieutenant was in the wrong—my chief revealed to me that the lieutenant was never supposed to disclose information from the bank, being that he was on the board and my attorney was right there and ready to fight back with a discrimination case if I had lost my job.

Once again, Destiny Helpers had stepped into my life: my chief and my attorney, who was ready to fight for me when I didn't have any fight left within me. I was cleared. But here, once again, was the assassin trying to take everything away from me. And once again, I had the victory. For the next few months, I was able to rest in Psalm 46:10: *Stop striving and know that I am God.*

# CHAPTER 13

Being sued, having to declare bankruptcy, and losing the spa, left me in such a dark place. I was at the bottom. At least, I still had the fire department to fall back on.

After seven years with the department, I was now a fire investigator and doing well. Of course, the assassin had to rise up again, and like before, he used my husband.

Marc came at me with the same argument—either I had to join his religion or we would have to get a divorce. It was amazing how two people could love each other, yet our marriage was in a dark place because of our faith.

One night when we were getting ready for bed, I felt a darkness and coldness in our bedroom that I'd never felt before. Even though it felt different, I just thought it was because of the state of our marriage. I slipped into bed and dozed off, but not that much later, I woke up to a huge demon standing at the foot of our bed. I stared at the demon, but he didn't back away. I began to plead the blood of Jesus over the room.

Even with my prayers, the demon didn't move and now, I was afraid. Marc was asleep beside me, but I was filled with the same fear I'd felt in my bedroom as a child. I kept praying, kept pleading the blood of Jesus, but my prayers appeared to make the demon angrier. It felt as if the demon was growing, rising above me and I threw the covers over my head, continuing to pray. I never came from under those covers, but eventually, I fell asleep.

A few days later, Marc and I were in the bedroom and I noticed his eyes were filled with tears. This time, he spoke words he'd never said to me before.

"Kayle, Yeshua is asking me to sacrifice my family."

"What?" I asked. I'd heard what he said, but his words shocked me.

"I think Yeshua is telling me to sacrifice my family," he repeated. "If you can't follow me, as much as I love you and our children, it's time for me to leave."

Tears rolled down my cheeks and I understood the cold darkness that I'd felt in our bedroom. I knew this was the beginning of the end. "I can give you a whole lot of things in life," I told Marc, "but I cannot give you my soul."

This conversation kept going on for a few days, and the discussion intensified. The assassin's goal was to get me to choose another religion where God wouldn't be able to use me, but like I'd said during all the years of our marriage, that was never going to happen. After a few days of a constant battle, it was time. I finally agreed to give Marc a divorce. It was the right thing to do because as his wife, I couldn't fulfill his greatest desire.

Marc and I had been married for more than fifteen years, and it was finally coming to an end. We were both sad about it, but this was something we both had to do.

I told Marc, "If you can just allow me one year to find another place, I'll let you keep the house. I just need to get my stuff together."

Marc agreed and we worked out how we would support our children. Our daughter, who was in middle school and our son, who was in high school, were going to live with me, though they would still spend a lot of time with Marc. I was glad about that because he was a good father.

Once we agreed to divorce, I got to work, searching every day for a new place to live. The challenge was that this was 2009 and the housing market had just crashed. The market was bad and my credit was bad because of my bankruptcy. It was going to be difficult for me to have a fresh start with all of this against me—difficult, but not impossible.

For anyone else, there would have been no chance of buying a house. However, when the hands of God are upon your life, and when you have exceptional faith, the circumstances won't matter. There had not been a time in my life when God had not come through.

As I searched for a house, I was turned down by the banks about three or four times. During the crash, the financial institutions were not taking chances on anything or anybody.

However, I stayed in prayer, kept my faith, and then, my realtor found a house.

Now, when I say she found a house—it was in Coral Springs… and it was a beautiful home. Except, I cannot even tell you the color of the house, that's how filthy it was. The grass came up to my knees as we walked to the door, the driveway was layered with dirt and inside, the walls and the carpet were covered with soot because the owner didn't have any power on in the house, so he used the fireplace for light. The home was infested with insects and rodents—it was just a mess…at least that's how most people would have seen it. I'd been given eyes that saw what other called trash as a treasure.

The house was on the market because the owner was about to lose it. It had been originally owned by a school teacher who'd died and she'd left the house to her son. However, the son wasn't in a good place…he was on drugs.

From the moment I saw the house, I knew *this* was the home that God was blessing me with.

One afternoon after I picked my daughter up from school and drove to the house because there was something I had to do. When we arrived, my daughter's eyes opened wide.

"Do you want to get out and take a look?"

She shook her head. "No, Mama, no!"

"Okay, you stay right here," I said, not paying any attention to her tone. I could tell she thought I was crazy to think this would be a good place to live.

I got out of the car and walked up to the house. Then, after taking a deep breath, I began walking around it. God had told me to come here and walk around this house seven times. He told me to declare that the house was mine.

I did as God instructed, walking and declaring, "It is so in Jesus' name. I declare that this house is mine." There were so many reasons why someone looking at me at that moment would have thought what I was saying and doing didn't make any sense. However, 2 Corinthians 5:7 was in my heart. The Word of God says, *For we walk by faith, not by sight.*

When I got back into the car, my daughter's expression had not changed. She looked at me like she was wondering what in the world was going on with this mess of a house? However, those were only her thoughts because she couldn't see what I saw. I truly saw the treasure of this place that was priced way lower than what I believed would be its true value. The house was over three-thousand square feet, with a pool that was right in the middle of the U-squared house. It would be a beautiful place for us to live.

My realtor submitted my offer and when it was accepted, I knew I'd have to do something different with the bank to get the financing. I had been turned down so many times and I didn't want that to happen again.

I called my aunt, Sugar, because she had reached out to me when I began searching for a home. She knew what happened with my business, she was aware of my break-up with Marc and she asked me if I was serious about starting over.

"I'm very serious," I told her. "I'm looking forward to having a new start."

She appeared to be pleased with my answer. She said, "I promised your mom before she died, that I would help you if you ever needed it, but after all of these years, you haven't needed any help at all. If you need me now, though, I will sign for your house if you find one."

I thanked my aunt, but as I found different houses, I hadn't called her. This time, though, I knew that I had to; the Lord told me this was the time. Right away, my aunt agreed to help. Just like all the other times in my life when the enemy had put roadblocks in my path, He'd given me another Destiny Helper—my Aunt Sugar.

Even though she was going to help me with the loan, I still had to come up with the down payment and I had no money. I wasn't concerned, though. After God had brought me this far, I knew the down payment would work out, too.

Just days after my aunt agreed to help me, I received a call from a young lady who used to work for me at Dare II Be Different.

"Kayle," she said. "I'm opening up a new salon and I heard you have some equipment for sale. Can I come by and see what you have that I can buy?"

She was talking about all of the equipment I'd taken from Tranquility Day Spa. I'd stored everything with a friend and after I got that call, I sent out a text to others letting everyone know that I had equipment for sale. It only took me two days to sell just about everything...and get $10,000, exactly what I needed for the down payment for my house.

Once I had that money, my aunt, Sugar signed on the loan with me. As I waited for approval, I kept going over to the house that I knew was going to be my home with outdoor bleach and other supplies. I went to work cleaning up that mess. I went over there day after day, even though the bank had not yet approved the loan. That didn't matter. I was moving on faith and doing what I knew God wanted me to do.

I was there so much that the seller's realtor became concerned. She said, "I really don't want you cleaning like that because if you don't buy the house, I don't want to owe you anything."

I told her, "If I don't get this property, you will owe me nothing."

I kept cleaning until I was approved for the house. Finally, I had a new home. With my next paycheck, I hired someone to pressure-clean the outside. That investment was so worth it because once that was done, I didn't have to paint the house at all. The pressure-cleaning revealed that the house was a beautiful light shade of coral. Even the rocks in front of the house looked new.

That took care of the outside. Now, all I had to do was tackle the inside.

I had turned that pit into a palace and because I had that success, that became just another reason for the assassin to attack me. We had only been in the house for a short time when sewage backed up into the family room. That was not only a mess, but it made the house smell so bad.

The silver lining in that disaster was that with the insurance I received from that back-up, I was able to put all new wooden floors throughout the house. That disaster had turned into a blessing.

Once I was settled into the house, I felt as if my entire life was settled and I began to lose myself in God. I had been through so much and all I wanted was more of God. I wanted to just thank Him, praise Him, worship Him.

Every evening when I came home, I did what I had to do, then I'd shut down at six in the evening. From that point on, I wouldn't do anything but commune with God. I ran after Him, seeking Him with everything in me.

Even though Marc and I were now in separate homes, we were still not yet divorced. Marc had been bringing me the divorce papers, but I never did anything with them. It wasn't that I was trying to delay it; it was just that my total and complete focus was on the Lord.

I did this for so long that my children noticed and one day, my son came to me and asked, "Mom, you're not waiting for Dad, are you?"

I frowned, having no idea what he was talking about. "What do you mean?" I asked.

"You're not waiting to get back together with him, are you?"

"No, I'm not," I said, shaking my head.

"Good because you really should move on with your life, Mom. Why don't you go out sometimes?"

I took a moment to think about my son's words. I knew where he was coming from. My son didn't understand what he was seeing. I was home all the time and he interpreted that as me being stuck because I wasn't out mingling. "I go out," I told him. "I go to work and I go to church."

He looked at me, shook his head, and then left me alone. I'd shut down that conversation, but my son was right. What would it hurt for me to go out sometimes? Maybe I could go on a few dates. It wasn't like I was trying to get married.

I decided to really consider what my son said, but I wasn't going to rush into it. I would just keep my eyes open and not long after I had that conversation with my son, I met a firefighter at a concert that I went to with my cousin. He was from Miami-Dade and of course, he was tall and very handsome because the enemy would never send someone that I wasn't attracted to.

At first, we spent lots of time talking on the phone. Since we were both firefighters, we had a lot in common and we really became friends. I did like him, but I was really leery. I was at a place in my life where I was whole and I didn't want to bring anyone into my life who wasn't like me. Really, I was not only leery of him, but I was leery of me as well. I didn't want to go back to the place from where God had delivered me. So while I was speaking to him, I continued to seek the Lord.

It was a good time. I was getting used to being single again and getting used to spending a lot of time alone when my children were out of the house and with their father. I was fine because being alone gave me even more opportunity to seek God.

However, I began to notice something during the times when I was alone. At night, I'd go to sleep, but then suddenly, I'd awaken when I felt the mattress move as if someone was getting into the bed with me. I would immediately pray, but in the morning, I felt like I'd had intercourse. I wondered what was going on because at the time, I wasn't familiar with sexual demons.

It became almost a nightly thing. Every night I prayed and prayed, but the spirits kept coming and I could even feel them touching me. No matter how much I prayed, those spirits wouldn't go away.

As this continued, I tried to think of things I could do and decided that maybe it would be good for me to go out with the firefighter. Maybe going on a date would keep those demons away.

The next time we spoke on the phone, I told him that I wanted to get together and he agreed. We made a date to meet after one of his shifts at an IHOP since he'd just be getting off from work.

The morning of our meeting, I drove into the parking lot and he was already there, sitting in his car. We waved to each other before he jumped out of his car and slid into mine. We had talked on the phone so much, that we just sat there and fell into a comfortable conversation. Then, he turned the discussion to sexual things. As I sat there listening to him, all of a sudden, I saw a spirit come out of his face before it quickly went right back inside of him.

With everything I'd been through, I knew what I was seeing. The assassin was showing himself to me; he was sitting inside this guy. What was shocking, though, was that I didn't leave. I didn't push him out of my car, I didn't tell him that I couldn't see him again.

Instead, I just continued to sit there. My challenge was that I was dealing with the spirit of loneliness. Two years had passed since Marc and I had separated and I guessed my son was right. I did want to get out more and now, I was committed to moving on. So instead of running, which is what I should have done, I not only stayed in the car, but when he said, "So, are you ready to get something to eat?" I went right into IHOP with him. We sat at a booth, had breakfast, and talked some more.

When we finally left the restaurant, we made plans to see each other again. I had seen the assassin inside of him, but I didn't want to stop our friendship. I was very much aware of the darkness that was in my presence, but what I was doing was what so many women (and maybe some men, too) do—we will override what the spirit of God is saying to us. God was speaking, even showing me the assassin. However, I wasn't listening because I was lonely and the enemy had sent me a man I was attracted to. That made it easy for me to ignore what was literally right in front of my face. I ignored the enemy in front of me for about eight months, and then, I finally fell into the enemy's trap.

I knew exactly what I was doing that night with the firefighter. I was trying to fill a void that hadn't been filled since Marc and I separated. I hadn't been with another man until that time. It wasn't that I wanted a relationship with the firefighter. What I wanted was a moment of companionship. So after eight months, it was very easy for me to fall. Not only had I slipped, but I slipped with the kingdom of darkness.

Not too many Sundays after that night, I was in church and I felt the strong anointing in that sanctuary. I was rejoicing in the Lord as I stood and praised and worshipped God.

Then, all of a sudden, I felt a stirring in my belly that stunned me. I stood there shocked for a moment. Was I pregnant? Right away, I said no. I knew what being pregnant felt like. Still, something was going on. It felt as if something was leaping inside of me.

This was not of God; this was not the Holy Ghost. I knew this was about the fact that I had slipped off into sin. Standing there in the sanctuary, I laid my hands on my stomach and prayed. After the service I went home, got on my knees, repented and cried. I cried so much, trying to rid myself of the guilt I felt.

The next time I spoke to the fireman, I told him that I wouldn't be able to see him again. I told him I had work to do for God, and asked him to please not call me anymore.

That was the end of one chapter and the beginning of another one.

# CHAPTER 14

Once again, I returned to diligently seeking God, and at that time, my cousin introduced me to her prayer line. The line which began at five-thirty every morning was called *The Watchers on the Wall* and was orchestrated by Bishop Shandra Robertson. She was such a strong woman of God and after listening to her speak, the ten or so of us who were on the line with her, took turns praying. It didn't matter to me how many of us were on the line, I would pray. I would pray to the point where I felt like I was being lifted up.

One morning, it was my turn to pray and I was praying so hard, I didn't hear anything. When I finished, I heard another woman on the line chanting, "The blood of Jesus, the blood of Jesus, the blood of Jesus." It was like a warfare prayer.

I didn't know why she was praying that way and when I asked her, she said, "You didn't hear that?"

"Hear what?"

"There was a demon speaking on the line. He was roaring."

"What? I was praying, I didn't even hear that."

In the next moment, I realized that again, the assassin was showing himself to me and now, he was angry. He was trying to get me to think there was something wrong with me—while Kayle is praying, let me disrupt the line.

It didn't work. All that did was make me keep praying harder. You see, at this point, I was really coming into the complete knowledge of who I was in Christ. I began to understand that there had to be something so valuable in me that the enemy had to lodge a serious attack.

That was why the enemy returned with those spirits visiting me nightly, overwhelming me with sexual feelings. In the morning, I felt so violated and I didn't know what to do. Even though I was back on track with God, I was in a spiritual battle that I didn't quite understand. That was part of my challenge; I needed to understand what I was fighting so that when I felt the spirits around me, I could stand up boldly.

Night after night, the spirits came. I'd keep my eyes shut and pray and pray. However, the spirits never went away. One night, I opened my eyes for a brief moment and saw the face of a woman in the bed with me. A woman? I'd never been with a woman in my life. I wasn't a lesbian, but seeing the face of that spirit made me feel worse and confused me even more. The confusion didn't end there because one night, I'd see a man and then, the next night, I'd see a woman. Later, when I learned to take authority over the spirits, I also learned that they were interchangeable.

At that time, though, not knowing that, I felt like I was really messed up. I began to feel as if I didn't even know who

I was. I started questioning myself: Was I really saved? Had I really been delivered? It was almost as if the spirits knew that if they got into my thoughts, I would be too confused to figure it out and take control.

The images of the spirits became even more absurd. One night, I saw a man in human form, dressed like a man, except his ears were shaped like a pig's. I prayed as I watched that spirit circle around my bed and then, he began to remove his clothes.

By this point, I was shaking, but in that moment, I remembered God's words in Luke 10:19: *I have given you authority to trample on snakes and scorpions and to overcome all the power of the enemy; nothing will harm you.*

I thought about those words. I had *authority*. That meant that I had to set up boldly before the demons. I had to be bolder in my spirit.

As the demon undressed, I sat up. This time, I wasn't going to play a telepathic mind game with the enemy. This time I spoke the Word of God aloud. That was the way to move that demon because demons knew the logos of God; demons knew that God's Word moved everything.

My flesh may have been shaking but my spirit was sound and I began to speak so boldly to that demon as if I was in a battle with him. I spoke as if he was a real person sitting before me.

"You are not welcome here and I rebuke you in the name of Jesus! So, get out and don't you come back!"

The Holy boldness of God stood up in me and my authority was released.

The demon obeyed and left. He disappeared because I'd stood up. To that point, I'd been fearful and weak, which is exactly the kind of personality a demon will prey on. That's why the demons had been able to traumatize me in the past.

Behaving that way that night taught me something. I learned that those demons were really cowards who knew that the light of God covered the darkness. In the end, after doing that night after night for about four or five years, I was able to get rid of the demons.

What a lesson that was for me. We have absolute power and authority over the enemy. It is clearly written in the Word of God and Jesus Himself told us that more than 2,000 years ago.

Here's the thing about demons, though. They may run, but they will always come back to test you and try you. They are persistent, never giving up. That's why you have to understand that your battle is in the spiritual realm. I finally learned that and I always stayed bold.

The enemy manifested itself not only mentally, but the assassin tried to attack me physically. One day, I suddenly got all of these flu-like symptoms. As the days passed, my symptoms worsened and I became really sick. Finally, I didn't have any other choice—I had to go to the doctor. After checking me out, he called in a few prescriptions for me.

I went straight home so that I could rest and one of my spiritual sisters came over, got the prescriptions and said she'd picked them up from the pharmacist for me. When she left, I got in bed and as I lay there, I began to pray. I said, "Raphael, you've got to bring the medicine."

As I lay there, flat on my back, my feet began to tingle (like they had fallen asleep) and then that feeling slowly rose through my body. I had no fear, I felt the peace of God. I just stayed still, knowing the Holy Ghost was doing something.

That feeling continued, rising in me. By the time that feeling touched the top of my head, it was like I had never been sick. Every symptom was gone!

When my spiritual sister knocked on my door with the medicine, I told her I didn't even need it anymore. I had just had a spiritual visitation and God had touched my body.

Now, I knew what Matthew 28:20 meant when God said: *I will be with you always, even until the end of the world.* I understood those words perfectly. Now, I knew that even when darkness came, God would bring His light. He would always be with me.

# CHAPTER 15

One day I was sitting in my car praying in regards to my marriage. It had been just over two years and Marc was on me about the divorce papers. I still refused to deal with them until I heard the voice of God speak.

That day, soaking in deep prayer, I heard the Lord say, *"It's time."* With a moment of comfort and peace, I called Apostle Dillard and said, "You don't have to pray another prayer for my marriage. God has spoken."

A few weeks later, one of my coworkers told me she'd met a really nice guy. "He's really spiritual," she said. "And I told him about you." The way I looked at her made her add, "I know you don't want to talk to guys or whatever, but just as a friend, I think it would be good for the two of you to meet. He wants to talk to you about the Word of God."

"Sure," I finally said. "Give him my number. Maybe I can invite him to church."

That was all I was thinking about. When he finally called, I thought my coworker was right. Etsy seemed to be very nice over the phone. He was mild mannered and sweet and just like my friend said, he was very spiritual. Our conversations were mostly about Jesus, about revelation, and the spirit of God. We just talked; he never came onto me and he never asked me anything personal.

I was glad about that because I really was in a new place spiritually. I had fallen in love with Jesus and I was so focused on becoming the woman that so many people had prophesied and said that I would become.

Etsy did tell me a little about himself. He was from Africa and he shared something personal with me, "I was a twin, but my twin died. When that happened, there were black birds all over our roof."

"Wow! Why was that? Why were the birds there?"

"That was a sign that I was spiritually gifted."

One day, our conversation turned to the end times and Etsy told me, "You have a job to do because the end times are here and most Christians don't even know who God really is. They have a form of godliness, but that's not you. Just talking to you, I can see your heart, and that's why I'm sure God is going to use you mightily in the end times." Then, he told me he operated in the gift of healing.

"Oh, that's good," I said. I'd always been intrigued with the supernatural and I loved hearing stories about miracles, signs and wonders.

He went on to tell me about a woman who had cancer and how he'd laid hands on her and she was healed. "I want her to tell you about that," he said. "I want you to know that I have this gift."

"Wow, that's a blessing," I said.

Etsy continued, "It is a blessing to be able to heal. That's why I want to get into the hospitals. I want to heal people in there and I was thinking that you can help me get access because you're a firefighter. And once I'm inside the hospitals, I can show you what God can do. You and I can do great work together."

I just let Etsy talk, but at first, I didn't respond to what he was saying. Yes, I worked for the fire department, but I wasn't going to jeopardize my job by giving him access to the hospitals. No way.

Finally I told Etsy, "No, you can do that on your own. I'm sure if you're going to pray for people, the hospital will let you in."

"But there's something about you. I'm telling you if we team up, God is going to do some miraculous work. We should go into the hospitals together."

Again, I told him he could do it; he could go to the hospitals and tell the administrators he wanted to pray for people. I never did tell him that I had access and I could have gotten him in.

It didn't seem to bother him that I wasn't willing to help in that way. He still wanted me to speak to the woman he'd healed. She called me and told me of her experience with stage four cancer and how Etsy had prayed for her, laid hands on her, and she was instantly healed. Then, she went on to tell me about her child.

"I have a daughter," she said. "And whenever my little girl sees him, she doesn't call him by his name. She calls him Gabriel."

The way she told her story, I was so happy and excited for her and grateful for what Etsy had done. After speaking to her, I enjoyed speaking with him even more and hearing about his gifts.

Then one day, I said to him, "You know what? I want to put a face to the voice on the phone. I want to meet you."

"Okay," he agreed.

We made plans to meet at the mall where I used to have my spa. I called my cousin, who was a pastor, and asked him to go with me to the meeting. He agreed and when we got to the mall, I looked around in the crowd for a face that matched the voice. Etsy was African, so I was looking for an African American.

Then, I heard a soft voice behind me. "Kayle?"

I turned around and was so surprised when I faced the man. The voice I had in my head made me think I would be meeting a very well educated African American man. However, that was not who stood in front of me.

"Nice to meet you," the very buffed, Spanish-looking man said. I had expected Etsy to be dressed conservatively, but he was wearing a tank top that showed his tattoos on both shoulders: one was a dog head with a human body and the other was an eagle head with a human body. I thought the tattoos were spiritually related, but I wasn't sure.

My cousin, who was a walking Bible and theologian, knew exactly what the tattoos meant. He was glowing when he asked Etsy, "Why would you have those false gods as tattoos on your arms?"

False gods? That was surprising to me.

Etsy said, "When I was younger, my parents had the tattoos put on me. They put them there for my protection."

My cousin shook his head. "That wasn't good," he said, as he went on to explain what each of those tattoos meant.

Even though I could tell that my cousin wasn't feeling this meeting, we still went into the restaurant attached to the mall. We sat and after we chatted for a little while, Etsy said something that he'd already said to me a few times, "Your heart. God gave you that heart and you're going to help many people because of it. But you have to be careful with the heart that you have." Then, he turned to my cousin and said, "You need to stop doing what you're doing."

My cousin and I frowned. My cousin said, "I don't know what you're talking about."

Etsy said, "I don't want to argue or anything. I'm just telling you, the drinking and the stuff you're doing is not good for you because I can see through you."

I could tell that Etsy's words rattled my cousin. He shook his head. "I don't do that anymore," he protested and kept repeating those words.

However, Etsy wasn't moved by what my cousin was saying.

He kept telling him that he had to stop.

My cousin looked at me and now, both of us were uncomfortable. "Let's go," my cousin said. "We don't need to sit here talking to this demon."

I got up with my cousin; I was ready to leave, too. So, I said goodbye to Etsy, thinking this had really been a strange encounter. That was the last time I saw Etsy...but that wasn't the last time I talked to him.

We continued speaking on the phone because I enjoyed that part of our friendship, but then one night, the conversation turned.

Etsy said to me, "Kayle, I have to tell you something, but I already feel like you're not going to receive it. But I have to tell you because there's work that we have to do together."

"Okay," I said. "Just tell me what you have to say."

After a moment, he said, "I'm not human."

"What? What do you mean?"

"I don't even eat human food."

"What do you mean by that?"

"The only way to explain it is what I already said—I'm not a human."

"I still don't understand what this means."

"I knew it would be very hard for you to accept it. But most humans call me Gabriel."

I hesitated for a moment. "Oh, my goodness," I finally said.

He said, "I only really come out at night."

Now, I said to myself, 'What in the world?' But even after that "revelation," I kept talking to Etsy. I wasn't sure why, but I wasn't afraid of him.

The phone calls between Etsy and I finally stopped though, when a few days after he revealed himself to me, my spiritual mother called me at work. Right away, I could tell she was very upset. Apostle Dillard was almost screaming, "Baby, where are you?"

"I'm at work."

"Who is this man that you're talking to?" she asked me. Before I could answer, she added, "You cannot have another conversation with him. This man is Satan himself who has come to kill you."

I sat back in my chair, then told the Apostle Dillard a little about Etsy. She told me to always be careful because there were three ways the enemy would come after me concerning my life with Christ.

The first way was through my character. She said, "That's why it's imperative that you be a good steward over the investment that God has made in you because if your character is off, if you're not walking in the character of Christ, then people won't accept the message you're sharing because you will have no integrity. People won't listen to someone with ill character."

Then, she said, "The second thing Satan will go after is your health. The enemy knows that if he is able to disable you,

you will not effectively be able to spread the good news about the kingdom of God. If your body is weakened, you won't be able to keep your mind on Christ." Finally, she finished with, "The third line of attack will come in the form of your finances. If you're not able to financially do what you have to do in the kingdom of God, then it will delay the actions that you're supposed to take."

I listened to all that she told me. Character, health and finances…from that point forward, those three areas would be where I would pay particular attention.

After I talked to the Apostle Dillard, I knew I couldn't talk to Etsy anymore. When he called me again, I politely told him we would never have another conversation.

He said, "I knew it. You're just like the other Christians. I knew you wouldn't believe."

It was amazing. I had been in the middle of that darkness again, but like all the other times, the favor of God was still upon me. If it were not for God, I would have been killed a long time ago. It seemed, though, as if I couldn't be touched because the enemy couldn't destroy everything valuable that God had placed inside of me. Because I was the Lord's investment, I had a legion of angels, warring angels who were in the battle on my behalf.

However, I was bothered by the whole Etsy situation. I had been on the phone having long conversations with the assassin, and I hadn't known it. I didn't have a discerning spirit. In Matthew 7:15, the Lord tells us, *Beware of the false prophets, who come to you in sheep's clothing, but inwardly are ravenous wolves.*

Etsy was that ravenous wolf. He seemed to know a lot, which was how he got me. I had been seeking God like never before, but I was still immature in the realm of the spirit. However, God made sure that I had that discerning spirit around me and even to this day, I thank Him for Apostle Dillard.

# CHAPTER 16

I felt as if I was coming into my own in the ministry and I was doing wonderfully. I attended Christian conferences, events and meetings as much as I could. I wanted to be around God's people. However, something very interesting was going on whenever I attended one of these events; I'd meet prophets who continually said the same thing to me.

"Woman of God, I don't know your name, but I just want to let you know, you're getting ready to marry a pastor."

At another conference, someone else would say, "Woman of God, I just want to let you know you're getting ready for marriage and God is going to do something miraculous in this union and in this ministry."

No matter where I went, I kept getting these prophecies. A woman even contacted me through my cousin. She had told my cousin that she really needed to speak to me because she saw me marrying a man. When she called me, she explained what she'd told my cousin and then, she described the man that God had shown her. "He's six feet tall, dark-skinned and bald, but I can't really see his features. All I know is that he's on his way."

No matter who would tell me this, I would smile and say thank you, but inside the assassin spoke to me in a loud voice. He was telling me, "No, no, no! You don't want that. Remember what happened the last time you were married? You don't want to be married. What if he's like your last husband or the other guys?"

I couldn't see what the prophets were saying because I kept telling myself that I didn't want to be married. I thought I had a good reason for saying that, too...I felt like I was whole. I had no appetite, no urge for sex. My flesh was 100 percent under subjection to the Word of God and I was fine with that. I was into the Lord and I felt like I was home!

However, because of all of these prophecies, I went to God and prayed: "I did not ask for a husband. But, if it is from you, let me see him." And then, I began to pray specifically because if God was going to send me a husband, there were certain things that I wanted in that man: I didn't want him to be shorter than six feet, I wanted him to be Godly, I wanted him to love the Lord...and all other kinds of things.

When I began praying that way, the assassin was still in my head telling me that I didn't want any of that.

A few weeks later, I got a call from one of my very good friends, Vienna.

She said, "Kayle, I have a friend. And he is very spiritual just like you. I know you're all about God, I know what you believe and how you don't do pre-marital sex. But he's a minister, too." She must have been able to tell that I was doubtful because she added, "I promise that you'll like him."

"You know what, Vienna, I don't know," I said, still indecisive.

She kept pressing me and I kept telling her no. But then, I heard the Holy Ghost say: "*What would it hurt just to talk to him?*"

I said, "Okay, God." And then, I told Vienna that she could give him my number.

A couple of days later, I got a phone call from this man who, right away, I thought was so sweet. "Kayle," he said. "My name is Clarence and Vienna said that I could call you."

"Okay."

We began to talk and of course, at that time, I couldn't see the gift that God was giving to me. I had no idea that this man would be another Destiny Helper who was coming to me in the form of a warrior. I couldn't see it because although I felt whole, in so many ways, I was so broken. I couldn't even see what God was doing. So I was a little hard with Clarence at first; there was no way I was going to let my guard down.

Still, I talked to him and Clarence told me all kinds of things about himself. He'd been in Georgia, but the Lord had sent him to Florida, back to the ministry where he used to pastor. "The Lord told me to go back there and lead the people," Clarence told me. "And the Lord also told me that my wife was there, too."

*Oh, that's nice*, I thought. I was happy for him.

After we'd been talking for a few months, he invited me to hear him preach at a church in Hollywood. So my cousin and I went down to the church and when we got inside, I realized I didn't even know who he was or what he looked like, but I knew he was a guest speaker.

My cousin and I looked around through the sanctuary. "He said he was going to be wearing a white suit," I told my cousin and I finally spotted him—an older gentleman, bent over a guitar. I pointed him out to my cousin and said, "He's not my type and I'm not going to play with a man of God."

I sat there and listened for a while, but I told my cousin that I didn't even want to stay. As soon as he got close to the end of the sermon, we left.

I jumped in my car and we left. Later that night, Clarence called and the first thing he asked was, "Kayle, why did you leave?"

I was surprised that he even knew that I was there. He didn't know what I looked like either, but then, Clarence told me that the Holy Ghost had revealed to him who I was not long after my cousin and I arrived.

Since he knew I'd been there, I had to come up with an excuse. "Oh, I was tired."

When he said he wanted to take me out to dinner, I said, "Okay," since I hadn't stayed to meet him. But I still wasn't feeling him. He was a nice man and we had good conversations, but like I said, he wasn't my type.

Looking back on this situation, I realize that God had so much work to do with me. I was like an onion that needed the layers pulled back. I was superficial, I was materialistic and in that moment, I couldn't see the man, I could only think that he wasn't my type.

Clarence and I went out to dinner and just like all the other times, I enjoyed talking to him. We both loved God so much and could talk about the Lord for hours. In our conversations, I was being fed emotionally as well as spiritually. God had sent me a man who could pray for me and protect me in the physical and spiritual realm. However, I didn't look at Clarence as the man that all the prophets were telling me about. I didn't see him that way because the scales were still on my eyes. I was still walking in the superficial.

Still, I continued to go out with him because I loved speaking with him and I felt like we were becoming good friends. Then, on Super Bowl Sunday, our relationship shifted a bit.

I was having my family over for the game and I invited Clarence to come as well since we were friends. Everyone was already at my house when Clarence walked in and I introduced him. I saw the shocked expressions on everyone's faces and I knew what everyone was thinking—this man is with Kayle? He wasn't anything like the men my family were used to seeing with me.

At first, my family wasn't very welcoming, but in my relatives' defense, they were all very protective of me. I was an independent woman with a professional career, my own house, my own Lexus—they were concerned with who was coming into my life. They didn't want anyone walking in trying to take advantage of me.

Even though they weren't friendly at first, that didn't bother Clarence. He was the type of man who could fit in wherever he went. So after he was introduced, he just sat down with the guys and started talking about the football game. He wasn't much of a football fan, but on that Sunday, you couldn't tell.

Football talk was all it took with the men. They warmed up quickly after that. It was the women who stayed back and watched him. After a couple of hours, though, Clarence had won the women over, too. Everyone really liked him.

I was so glad about that because Clarence was a good man and I wanted us to remain friends. The scales were still on my eyes. I didn't see the protection God had placed in my life because of where the Lord was taking me. With the plans He had for me, I needed a protector in the natural because of where God was taking me spiritually. At least, I did enjoy his company and we continued to go out together.

One night, after we returned from dinner, Clarence pulled his car to a stop in front of my house and after a moment, he turned to me. I was shocked to see the tears that rolled down his cheeks.

In the same gentle voice with which he always spoke, he said, "The Lord has spoken to me. As I was driving from

Georgia to Florida, the Lord told me that my wife was in Florida."

I nodded; Clarence had told me that before.

He continued, "And when I saw you at the church, the night that you left, the Lord told me then that you were going to be my wife."

I was shocked. "The Lord told you that I'm your wife?" I wondered how could this be happening when I hadn't even known this man a year.

He nodded. "That's what the Lord said. Kayle, we've been talking for months now, but if you can't see yourself loving me, then allow me to leave now."

I sat there frozen, wanting to feel something because of what he'd just told me. But I didn't feel anything. Inside, I kept praying, "God, if this is you, allow me to feel something."

However, no matter how many times I said that, I still felt nothing for this sweet man.

Finally, I did the only thing I could do. I told Clarence good night, then I got out of the car. I didn't look back as I walked to my house and when I stepped inside, I put down everything, went straight into my bedroom and then right beside my bed, I dropped to my knees.

"Lord, I don't want to go against Your will. But if this is the man of God that you told me about, you've got to speak to me."

I stayed on my knees and I prayed and I cried. Then, I cried and I prayed. I stayed on my knees because I really wanted to seek the will of God; I really needed to hear from Him.

Finally, I heard the Lord speak in a stern voice. He said, "*I ordained it!*"

As soon as I heard God, the walls around me crumbled, the scales fell from my eyes and the peace of God rested upon me. Once God spoke to me, I put my heart into what He had told me. I started fully dating Clarence. With every conversation, I felt a little more peace because I was holding onto God.

Four or five months later, Clarence told me he was going to my spiritual mother since both of my parents had passed away. He called my Destiny Helper and asked Apostle Dillard for my hand in marriage.

She told him, "Yes!" and then, she called me. "He's a good man of God, Kayle." With those words, my peace was complete.

In 2013, Clarence and I were married and as we took our vows, I knew the Holy Ghost was there.

# CHAPTER 17

Once we were married, it became clear to me that God was calling me a little bit higher. I had just married a pastor, so now, I was an Elect Lady and I began seeing the world differently. The battles were still coming, I still found myself in spiritual warfare, but with my husband by my side, I had reinforcement. Not only had I married a prophet and a prayer warrior, but Bishop was also a seer, one who could see angels and demons and he could war with authority in the spirit.

Every morning, my husband would say something to me like, "Okay, we have two angels in front of us and two on the side. I see them, Kayle, they're out there."

Just those words made me feel so secure. God had really put me in a safe place. But just because I'd been placed in the presence of a prayer warrior, that wouldn't keep the enemy away permanently.

One night, not too long after Bishop and I married, I was already in bed when the Lord said to me, "Tie the prayer shawl around your shoulders and go into the other room."

Following the Lord's instructions, I got out of bed. Inside the guest bedroom, I laid down and fell asleep, but it was a light sleep because not too much time passed before I awakened. However, when I opened my eyes, I couldn't move and I couldn't speak. A heavy darkness weighed down upon me. All of a sudden, chaos erupted: mirrors fell, furniture broke apart, debris flew through the air. It was as if a hurricane had hit the room.

I watched all of this going around me, but I was helpless. I still couldn't move, couldn't speak. Then, in the middle of this chaos, a short man appeared in front of me. As he moved toward me, there was nothing that I could do to get away.

Then, something I'd never felt before happened. It was as if my spirit man rose up out of me and spoke in a tongue that I'd never heard. I watched that man back up, then turn around and try to get away. I watched in awe at something else I'd never seen before. Instead of the spirit just disappearing, it appeared as if that demon was trying to use the doorknob to get out of the room. In the next moment, there was a loud boom! Then, nothing but silence.

For a minute or so, I laid there, looking around as the quiet settled all around me and I no longer felt paralyzed. Finally, I got up and ran back into my own bedroom.

Bishop and I had been married for more than three years when I began helping a woman who wanted to open a church.

She said she was an apostle and because I loved God, I loved His church and I loved His people, I wanted to do everything I could to help her.

She was opening a church in a storefront and as a fire inspector, (and she was in my zone) I could give her the help and guidance she needed to make sure her space was up to code.

I had just started helping this woman when I lost something that was very valuable to me—I lost a key to a valuable box that I owned. At the first sign that I had misplaced it, I searched everywhere. But no matter where I looked or for how long, I couldn't find it. So, I set that thought aside, thinking that I had just lost it forever.

Not too many nights after that, I had to return to my office for something that I'd left there during the day. Bishop was with me and as we drove up to the building, I saw a dark disfigured spirit standing by the door.

My first thought was that I didn't walk in the spirit of fear. Plus, my husband, and mighty warrior was by my side. So I entered the building without giving it another thought. Had I known what kind of demonic force had been standing there, I wouldn't have entered that door.

However, I did go inside, got what I needed and then, we left. Not too many days after that, I was standing at my desk and when I leaned over my computer, it felt as if every pore in my body opened. I knew this was spiritual, but I'd been through so many of these encounters that I just brushed it off, not thinking too much about it.

So over that time span, I'd met that woman who said she was an apostle, lost something that was valuable to me, saw that demon standing at the door of my office building and then, had that encounter at my desk. The next day, a demonic door opened up in my life like nothing I'd ever seen.

I was sitting at my desk when I began to feel things crawling all over me, crawling in my hair, crawling under my feet. I felt snakes wrapping around me. However, whenever I looked at my arms or my legs, I didn't see anything. At first, I just brushed my body, wondering what was happening.

For about three or four days, I didn't even mention this to anyone. I just prayed and consulted God, asking Him what was happening to me? This didn't make sense. Not only was I whole, but I was married to a powerful man of God, a prayer warrior who was able to pick this stuff up in the realm of the spirit.

It continued for so many days that I finally told Bishop about it. As I described what was happening, my husband was quiet, at first. It was as if he wanted to really listen because he didn't understand. When I finished, we prayed together and I felt a bit of relief after his prayer. However, it continued and every day it seemed to intensify and get worse.

I went to my spiritual mother since even with our prayers, nothing was changing. I hoped Apostle Dillard could give us reinforcement.

"I don't know what's happening," I told the Apostle. I began to tell her all that I was feeling and coming up against.

Apostle Dillard prayed over me and then, she told me some things to do, some things that I could bathe in.

I followed what she said, but still, it continued. Now, when I sat in the car, I felt snakes under my feet and wrapping around my stomach. It was too much. In the natural, I hated bugs. So the enemy was attacking me with something that I hated.

Every day my husband and I prayed and prayed, yet the attack continued. After weeks passed, I felt like I was about to lose my mind. Everyone was praying, everyone was at war for me, and I wasn't getting better. As more time passed, I felt as if I was fighting for my life.

One night at a church revival service, I was sitting in the pulpit with the other leaders. The lady who was praying, paused for a moment before she said, "Who is this with the witchcraft on them so bad?"

Her eyes were on the congregation in front of her, but I was in the pulpit behind her.

So, I stood up. She turned around and gazed at me. "Oh, my God. I almost need to take your clothes off." She said, "I need to throw oil down your throat and all over you."

I was so desperate at that point that I said, "I don't even care if you take my clothes off in front of the people. I am desperate to come out of this." Even then, as I was speaking to her, I felt something crawling all over me.

She motioned for me to come down from where I was sitting and she poured oil over me, from my head to my toes.

When I left the church that night, I was filled with such hope, but just like everything else, it was to no avail. The assassin was going in for the final kill.

Day after day, it continued. Day after day, it worsened. Now, I didn't only feel creatures crawling on me, but I felt things hanging from my eyelashes and my face. I felt it, but without being able to see it, I didn't know how to win this spiritual battle.

I prayed to God asking Him what to do. "What is this, God?" I kept asking over and over. It became impossible for me to even sit still. How could I with things constantly crawling over every part of my body.

In church, I shared with a few people what had been going on with me, and everyone joined us in prayer. However, no matter how many people prayed or laid hands on me, nothing changed.

I was functioning, going to work, working in our church, and still helping the woman with her church. Yet, I was miserable.

One day during my lunch break, I drove out to the lake and as I sat there, I cried and prayed. I told God, "If you don't come and do something about this, I'm going to die." As I prayed, I saw my children's faces flashing before me and I didn't know what that meant. "God, what is happening to me?" I wanted to know why had this spiritual wickedness come for me. Who had sent these demons? As I spoke to God, I was so distraught because I felt hopeless and helpless.

Sitting there at the lake, I felt as if I had my first answer to my prayers. God said, "*The devil is trying to take your mind, and I'm allowing you to experience hell on earth.*"

I left the lake, still without any kind of understanding. Actually, now I felt worse because now I couldn't figure out why God would want me to see hell on earth.

The days turned into weeks that became months and all I could do was cry out to God. I was desperate for deliverance and I sought out everyone, anyone who could help me. People prayed, they laid hands on me. I even searched for people who had this kind of anointing. People who could get this witchcraft off of me.

I knew one of the most important answers I needed to have was where was this coming from. Every day I asked God to reveal who was behind this. Who had me sitting under this demonic force?

However, God didn't speak to this question.

Months had passed and then, the enemy took it up a level. Now, the assassin took over my eye-gates. I didn't notice it until the day I drove by a billboard for Terminix. There were dozens of bugs all over the ad and a surge rushed through my body. The feeling I'd had for all these months intensified. I couldn't believe it could get worse, but it did. When driving, I had to avoid that route so that my eyes couldn't be used against me.

I prayed Psalm 144:1: *Blessed be the Lord, my rock, who trains my hands for war and my fingers for battle.* I needed the Lord to equip me because that would be the only way I'd win.

I knew at this point that I was fighting for my life. Of course, the feeling of those creatures on me wouldn't kill me, but the mental and emotional toll that it was taking on me would definitely take my life if something didn't change. At work, I began to think of other ways I could get relief. I wanted to go to the hospital and beg someone to shoot me in the head. That would give me peace, even if it was just for a few days or a few hours, even a few minutes. I needed to have relief or else I wanted to die.

I cried all the time and one morning when I'd pulled my car into the lot at work, I sat there for a few moments just crying. When my cell phone rang, I glanced at the screen, then answered it.

Apostle Dillard screamed, "Baby, where are you?" She sounded frantic and I told her I was at work.

She said, "I'm so sorry, but God just showed me that the witches have you in a coffin. They're trying to kill you. But God promised me that He will bring you out of it. But only you can walk it out for the anointing. You've got to walk it out."

It wasn't what I wanted to hear, but at least Apostle Dillard had given me a message that I could hold onto. Her words meant that God was going to deliver me; I was not going to die.

After that day, I knew God was going to bring me out, but that He wanted me to understand what He was doing. It didn't matter how many people would pray for me or lay hands on me.

God was showing me that He was the only one who could deliver me from this. Once He did, I would know that He was God.

This reminded me of the battle with Gideon when God had to show the people that He was Jehovah-Gibbor, the God of War.

I had hope, but it was still hard. Even knowing that God was trying to strengthen me through this, I didn't feel stronger in my faith. In fact, there were times when I felt like a child the way I was crying and whining. One day when I came home, Bishop looked at me and shouted, "Enough!"

As I wept, my husband stripped the bed and then he laid me down. He poured oil from my head to my feet. Then, he laid a Bible and a cross on me before he went to war in the spirit. After he prayed, he opened up the sliding doors in our bedroom and we heard: Boom! Boom! Boom! Then another sound like scuffling, as if someone…or something was rushing out.

"Kayle, oh, my God," my husband shouted. "She was half spider and half human."

I breathed with relief and prayed that it was over. That night when I closed my eyes, I rested for the first time in months. The next morning, when I awakened…there was nothing. I was hopeful as I returned to work…and then, I was right back in the web! There were snakes around my ankles, wrapping themselves around my stomach. There were things hanging from my eyes.

"God," I cried, totally not understanding the delay in my deliverance. What was going on? Hadn't my husband prayed last night? What about all the prayers from everyone else? I remembered that Apostle Dillard said I had to walk it out, but how much longer?

I was very much aware that the anointing came with a price. Abraham had to leave his home for a place that was revealed to him later. Noah was mocked and ridiculed when he followed God's instructions to build an ark. Moses had to give up a lavish lifestyle in Egypt to lead the Hebrew children. Yes, the anointing always came with a price, but I didn't know how much longer I'd be able to stay in this battle.

The war became so bad that my husband and I decided we'd have to leave our house. We had to get out of there. We put the house up for sale, but we didn't wait until it was sold. We packed, put our possessions into storage, and then, we went to stay in an Extended Stay hotel. Our plan was to be there until we moved into our new home.

It took us about two weeks to pack up everything and on the night when we finally had everything out of our home, we were exhausted when we got to the Extended Stay hotel. All we wanted to do was shower and get into bed.

After his shower, my husband laid down for a moment, but then, when he stood up, he collapsed. I ran over to him and got on my knees. "Clarence!" I kept calling his name. Then, I prayed over him.

I was trembling with fear. The darkness had followed us. As I prayed over my husband, I called Apostle Dillard.

After I told her what was going on, she tried to calm me down. "All right, Kayle," she said. "Baby, pray."

I prayed and prayed until Bishop sat up and then stood up. When I helped him up to the bed, I asked him if he wanted me to call 9-1-1.

"No, I'm fine, now," he told me.

I believed him because I knew I'd prayed him through. We were blessed, but still, the assassin had followed us from our home. I knew then that those demons weren't finished with me and I feared that he would now go after those who I loved.

# CHAPTER 18

After the attack in the hotel, Bishop and I left there and went to stay with friends who were gracious enough to open their home to us while we searched for another house. Just days later, I discovered that I'd been right about my concern. The assassin hadn't yet taken me out; he was going after my family.

When my daughter came to pick me up from work a few days later, she told me, "I don't know what it is, Mom, but whatever has been going on with you it's tried to jump on me. It feels like things are crawling on me." Then, she said, "But I said, 'oh no. That devil is a liar.'"

The same thing happened to Bishop. One day when we were in the car, my husband started tapping his head. "Something is crawling on my head," he said.

This was proof to me the assassin was touching people in my presence. I didn't know it was possible, but now, I prayed harder. My daughter had been right—the devil was a liar and I wasn't about to allow him to get close to those that I loved.

While the enemy went after my family, that didn't stop him from coming after me. Even moving out of our home didn't help and I continued to search for ways to fight the assassin. I decided to take a hyssop bath, which was going to be a seven-day cleansing and healing regiment. I'd use special soap and oils that were designed to purge negative elements from my mind and body; it was supposed to remove all manners of evil.

As I soaked in the tub that first night, I prayed Psalm 37 and Psalm 51 over my life and I cried out to God. "I can't take this anymore. Show me who this is! Show me!"

The next day, an Apostle who was a friend of one of my friends called me. My friend had told him what I'd been going through and he said, "The reason you're experiencing this thing daily is not because your prayers aren't working. You're still experiencing this because the witches are sending new demons every day to kill you. So as you bind and chain some, the next day a new set is released."

Now, I had a bit more understanding. The demons were coming daily. But there was one thing I still wanted to know—who had put this upon me? I felt as if I could answer that question, I'd be able to fight in the right way.

That night, after I took another bath, I knelt by the bed. All of a sudden, it felt as if a beehive was on my lower body. The bees were stinging me so badly that I jumped up and laid across the bed. All I could do was cry and beg God. I cried for so long that finally, I closed my eyes and fell asleep. Then, I had a vision. In my mind, I saw a woman sitting in a chair, but her head was cut off. The head was on the side of the chair, but the eyes inside the head were still moving.

Then, the Lord said, "*I severed the head of the enemy, but it's as if it's still moving.*"

I woke up and felt as if I was filled with the knowledge of what was happening. God was telling me that He had already cut off the head of the witch who had come after me. In Exodus 22:18, the Word of God says, *Thou shall not suffer a witch to live.*

God had already taken care of it and all I was feeling now was the residue. I was thankful for this message from God because that meant I was coming to the end of this battle. However, there was still one thing I wanted to know…who was behind this? When had it all started?

Right away, a thought came to me, but I tried to push it away. I couldn't ignore my thought for too long, though. This had all began when I started helping that woman. A woman who hid behind the name of an Apostle. I shook my head not wanting to believe it. There was no way someone was going around using the name of an apostle, but in truth, she was a witch.

I thought about her all night, though I didn't say anything about her to anyone. The next day, Bishop called me from work. He said, "Kayle, I was on the rooftop praying and I saw my face on a building."

At first, I didn't understand. My husband often prayed on the rooftop of one of the condos where he worked. But I didn't know what he meant when he said he'd seen his face.

He repeated it again and then, he said, "I saw my picture on the building and then, the Lord spoke to me and said *her* face is on the building."

So, I drove my vehicle to where my husband had been and when I arrived at the building, it wasn't my face that I saw—it was the woman I'd been thinking about…the woman who'd told me she was an Apostle, the woman I'd tried to help. Her picture was in the window of the building.

As I sat there staring, not able to believe what I was seeing, the Lord spoke to me. "*That is her.*"

She was the one who'd done all of this to me? Why? I didn't even know her.

God said, "*Helpers of the assassin.*"

Once God said that, something else came to me—my missing key. I'd lost the key right around the time that I'd met her and I knew witches needed something that belonged to the men and women they targeted. It *was* her!

But while I now had answers, the residue remained on me. I was still not relieved; I still felt those snakes and bugs all over me and then, on top of that on my drive home that day, I saw another one of those Terminix billboards.

I wanted to cry out, but then, the Holy Ghost said, "Curse the billboard."

Staring at that ad with all of those bugs, I did as the Lord guided. "I curse you in the name of Jesus. You will not be on another billboard, you spirit of hell!"

Over the next few weeks, the Terminix billboards were gone and I began to feel better. I didn't feel the bugs the way

I had, but my skin was sensitive. I could still feel things when I walked into certain rooms.

The Holy Ghost told me, *"Keep walking it out."*

That was all I could do—walk it out. It had been almost a year of torment that I knew was coming to an end. Still, it was hard with even the little bit I was feeling. I couldn't take much more.

The Lord said, *"My Hands are upon you."*

Every day, though, it became a little bit better…the only thing, I began dreaming of witches. However, even that came with a revelation.

I was told, *Once you identify the witch, and she knows that you are aware of who she is, you have taken their power. Now you have the anointing to destroy the works of the enemy.*

Slowly, I was coming back to myself. My eye-gates were back…things that I saw didn't bother me. My skin was back… still sensitive, but I didn't feel the bugs anymore. My sanity was back…I had walked it through and now I wanted to live and not die.

Once again, the enemy had been defeated. The assassin couldn't get my life. Even with reinforcements that the enemy had sent, there was nothing that could be done to take me out.

In my torture, I'd been spiritually awakened. Now, I wasn't just saying a prayer, I had been touched. I saw God in a totally different light.

I came to understand that the life I was living was not my own. I had been bought for a precious price and I totally belonged to God, Jehovah Gibbor. God had been mighty in my battle and I knew this personally. No longer was I hearing about the Lord through others. No longer was this about a sermon I'd heard. Now, I knew for myself because God had taken me through. I had been re-processed on the Potter's wheel and God was allowing me to reintroduce myself. What I'd gone through, this whole process had been necessary for me. 1 Peter 4:12-13 speaks of this: *Beloved do not be surprised at the fiery ordeal among you, which comes upon you for your testing, as though something strange were happening to you; but to the degree that you share the sufferings of Christ, keep on rejoicing, so that at the revelation of His glory you may also rejoice and be overjoyed.*

I'd seen God mighty in battle. I now knew Him to be the great I AM.

God had shwon me who He was, but the messages from the Lord didn't stop there. One night, as I laid down to rest, I closed my eyes, but I was in that state where I was between being awake and being fully in a deep sleep.

I saw myself standing in the middle of a line. There were several people in front of me, but even though the line wasn't long, I couldn't see the front. As the line kept moving, I kept looking, trying to determine what kind of line this was. Finally, I came close enough to the front to see what was going on.

There was a person in the front of the line passing out two garments to each person who stood in front of him. The garments were two long dresses: one with a wide belt and the other, a narrower belt.

Each person took their garments and then…like lightning, they shot straight up toward the heavens. That's when I realized I was in the heavenly realm. This was the entryway to heaven.

This was so exciting. I watched everyone in front of me get their garments and then shoot up. As I moved forward, my excitement increased. This was heaven.

When I got to the front of the line, though, I heard a deep voice resonate from my left. "Your name is not on the list."

I stood there, frozen. Because I was in the heavenly realm, I knew I wouldn't be speaking with my mouth. Communication wasn't audible. I only had to have a thought and it was answered.

Again, I turned to my left and again the deep voice repeated, "Your name is not on the list."

A knot cramped my stomach. 'Oh, God!' After all this time, I hadn't made it into heaven. I started to cry hysterically.

Then, on my right, I heard another voice. This one was much softer, much gentler. The voice said, "Your work is not done. You have not done the work."

Still, I was devastated as I got out of the line. I was still crying as I walked away from the line. I felt rejected. How had this happened? I hadn't made it into heaven and I didn't know what to do. I walked and walked, and then in front of me, I saw my daughter.

I felt the urge to minister to her soul. "Get your life in order," I told her as I cried. "You cannot be lukewarm. If you are, you're not going to make it into heaven. Heaven is nigh…heaven is nigh." I had to warn my daughter because I didn't want her to end up as broken as I felt. I wasn't going to heaven; I didn't want that to happen to her.

Seconds later, I came out of the heavenly vision. As soon as I opened my eyes, the assassin hit me with a thought: "You're not going to heaven. You're not going to make it in."

The same knot that I felt in my stomach in my vision came back and now, I was truly disturbed. I couldn't get that thought out of my head—I wasn't going to heaven.

Getting up, I went into the bathroom and there, I sobbed. I wanted to repent and I kept telling God that I was so sorry. "God," I cried out, "I cannot be left behind."

Even as I cried out to God, the assassin attacked me. "You're not going to heaven," he said over and over. "You're not going."

I was whole, I was in the knowledge of God, I knew about repentance and salvation. But still in that moment, the assassin was able to attack my mind because all I knew after waking from that vision was that I didn't want to be left behind, I didn't want to be lost.

After I got myself together, I went back to bed and slept through the night. In the morning when I awakened, Bishop was already gone, so I called one of my girlfriends, who was a prophetess. I just had to share my experience with someone.

After she listened to my whole vision, she said, "Oh my God, I wouldn't have wanted to have that dream."

Her words did not comfort me. So, we prayed together.

Then, I called another friend because I wanted to hear her thoughts. Even as I was telling her about it, I kept saying inside—God, I cannot be left behind, I cannot be lost.

The assassin kept coming, bombarding my mind with things God had already forgotten; God had already thrown my transgressions into the sea of forgiveness. He said that once you repent and become Godly sorry, He would remember those things no more. *Behold, you are now a new creature!*

I knew all of these things, but the assassin was relentless, telling me that I hadn't done what God had told me to do. "So you're not going to heaven. You didn't do the work. You didn't do the assignment."

The battle was so strong in my mind that I finally called my husband. "Babe," I said, "I've got to tell you what I experienced." He was silent as I told him everything.

But when I finished, he said, "I'm so glad you didn't accept the garments because if you had, I would be planning your funeral even now." He just kept saying over and over how glad he was that my vision ended the way it had.

As Bishop continued talking to me, I heard the Holy Ghost say, "*You must do the work.*" Now, I understood! There was more to be done; there were things I had to finish; I hadn't completed the task yet.

It took me speaking to my husband and the Holy Ghost coming to me to realize the message of the vision. It wasn't that I hadn't made it into heaven. The message was that I still had more work to do.

I thought about my vision more intently. I knew God and I heard His voice so clearly. Jesus said He sits on the right hand of the Father and the voice in my vision came from the right. It was the angel who keeps the Book of Life on the left saying that my name wasn't on the list. But he said my name wasn't on the list; the angel didn't say my name wasn't in the book. Jesus was on the right, telling me I had not yet done all the work.

Still, even though I came to an understanding, the enemy, Satan himself, tried to get inside of my mind to confuse me. The battlefield of the mind is real. The closer you get to Christ, the greater the battle becomes. The assassin had to raise the stakes because as I got closer to God, he had to try even harder to take me down.

I blocked out the assassin and kept my focus on the message: to just do the work. I had to do the work now, while I was alive because like John 9:4 says, *We must carry out the works of Him who sent Me as long as it is day; night is coming, when no one can work.* From that point, I came to the understanding of what God wanted from me. When He said to love thy neighbor, I now knew what to do. When He said for me to love my enemy, I now knew what to do. Now, I could forgive anyone who came up against me. I could forgive anybody the assassin used for my demise. I could forgive anybody who crossed me, who was jealous of me, who was deceitful to me. Why? Because God forgave me for everything and now my priority in life was to do the work.

Once I had that understanding, it was even easy for me to forgive the man who molested me and anyone else who had attacked me in my life. With this understanding, I was sure that now when I got back into that line, my garments would be presented to me and I would go up into glory.

I believe my vision was a message for everyone. When the assassin comes into your life to steal, kill and destroy, when he uses family members and friends against you, the most important thing that you must do—you *must* forgive them. That's part of the work. You have to take the face off the vessel, remove the face from the demon, so that you can love the soul. Always remember that it was not the person who came after you; it was the assassin who used someone you know.

I am aware that forgiving others is not an easy task. It wasn't easy for the disciples either. In Matthew 18:21, Peter asked the Lord how often should he forgive his brother who sinned against him?

Jesus answered, "*I do not say to you seven times, but seventy times seven.*"

So with that directive from Jesus, I will love my enemies. I will do that and so much more. I will do everything that God has asked of me. I will do the work because I don't want to miss heaven. I'm going to hold onto Romans 8:38-39:

*For I am convinced that neither death, nor life, nor angels, nor principalities, not things present, nor things to come, nor powers, nor height, nor depth, nor any other created thing will be able to separate us from the love of God which is in Christ Jesus our Lord.*

I receive that message from that vision and I accept the challenge.

# CHAPTER 19

I'd moved past all of that spiritual wickedness and my marriage with Bishop was going well. Of course, I was still dealing with the assassin, but now, my discernment had increased, my prayer life had increased, my mind was bound to the mind of Christ and my ears stayed pressed against God's lips. I was walking and living for Christ. It was not only because of what He'd done for me, but now, I had a full understanding of who God was. My life wasn't my own and I understood 1 Corinthians 6:20: *For you have been bought for a price: therefore glorify God in your body.* I'd been bought for a price and was the apple of God's eye.

God had set my husband and me up in a church and everything was going well...until Covid hit. I began preaching against that spirit, covering the people of God under the blood of Jesus.

I still had to work and was out in the field. While I protected myself, I told my husband that I came into contact with so many people who weren't wearing masks. The people weren't listening, they didn't think Covid was real. It troubled me, but there was nothing I could do about them. I could only control my own behavior and I constantly and consistently wore my mask.

Then, sitting at work one day, my head began to throb. The headache intensified through the day until I had the worst headache I'd ever had in my life. I had to hold my head to get some relief. Like always, I was used to these spiritual battles and demonic opposition, so I began to pray. However, the headache remained.

I went home and rested, but the next day, my head was still pounding. Even though I wasn't feeling well, I still went to work. Then, I was still at church, preaching and teaching against Covid, covering the people of God and myself with prayer. Still two days later, I still had that headache.

On the third day, I began having chest pains.

Now, I knew I needed additional covering. I called my husband at his job.

"I still have this headache," I told Bishop, "but now, my chest hurts. It feels like it's squeezing in. I can't figure out what's going on."

My husband and I began to pray while I sat there at my desk at work. We prayed again later when we both got home. I went to bed and returned to work the next day, even though I was starting to feel worse. I began to think that maybe I had a bad sinus infection. As I sat at my desk, I called my spiritual mother because I wanted to double up on my prayers. When I got her on the phone, I told her what was going on.

"Are you still at work?"

"Yes," I told her. I felt bad, but I had to do my job.

Apostle Dillard said, "I need you to go see about yourself because if you die, everything at the fire department is going to keep moving. You need to call your supervisor now and tell them that you're leaving; that you're not feeling well."

She was right and when I hung up, I did what she told me to do. When my supervisor answered, I told him, "I know you don't want to hear this right now, but I'm sick." I went on to explain how I'd been feeling and he was alarmed. "I think you need to get straight over to the hospital."

It was the sound of his voice that made me agree. My husband was at work and I didn't want to bother him with this right now. The doctor would probably just tell me that it was a bad sinus infection and then, he'd give me a prescription to fight it. So, I drove myself to the hospital.

When I arrived, my head seemed to be pounding even more and I was grateful that I didn't have to wait long for a nurse to see me and do a couple of tests.

After testing me, she said, "I don't know all that you've been doing, but I know you work for the fire department and I can tell you that you drank a big dose of Covid-19."

"What?" I was so shocked. How could this happen to me when I had not only been so careful, but I'd been praying and covering everyone.

She said, "What you're experiencing now are the first stages of pneumonia; that's why you're having chest pains."

This was not only hard for me to hear, but it was hard for me to believe. The medical team suggested that I stay at the hospital because they were concerned about my symptoms and the early stages of pneumonia. However, I wouldn't even consider that. I had to go home. That was my safe haven.

"Okay," the nurse said, "well, the only thing we can give you at this time is Tylenol. Would you like some?"

I was still in shock as I stared at her. I had been screaming Psalm 91, especially verses 9 and 10, at everyone: *For you have made the Lord, my refuge, The Most High, your dwelling place. No evil will happen to you, or will any plague come near your tent.*

Yet now, here I was. I hadn't even been thinking about Covid when I first got ill. I had been used to the enemy coming at me in one way and I wasn't at all prepared for this curve ball.

The first thing I did was call my husband with the devastating news. "I have to quarantine for the next fourteen days. I'm going to come home."

However, the next day, I wondered if I'd made a mistake. I still had the headache and the chest pains...and now, my lower back ached. I was declining.

Quickly, I realized that I didn't have enough fluids inside of my body; the coronavirus was drawing the fluids out of me and that was a major concern since I had a history of challenges with dehydration. I had to be careful; I didn't want my kidneys to shut down. I began to pray to God specifically about that.

While I continued to think about my situation spiritually, my training allowed me to also look at this medically. I reached out to a friend in the medical field and I told him that I needed an IV because I needed fluids in me. I knew that was why so many people died in the beginning.

Thank God for my friend, because he came over, masked up, and started an IV on me. Once I had those fluids intravenously, my prayer was that I'd start feeling better. After hours, though, I realized that wasn't happening.

I prayed, "Lord, you have to heal my body." It still didn't make sense to me that this was even happening. How could I pray against something so hard, pray and cover the people of God—and none of the people were infected with Covid-19, but here I was with this. No one else in my family, in the church were infected. How did this happen to me?

As I laid in the bed praying, it occurred to me that I hadn't heard from God. Since this all began, I'd been praying, but God had been silent. What was that about?

Each day, the symptoms continued and I wasn't getting better. My chest was contracting so much that it was tough for me to breathe. Becoming dehydrated and having that affect on my kidneys was still my major concern.

I remained in bed, not able to do much of anything. As I continued to decline, I began to think about my life: my children, my husband, our church. I told God, "If you take me now, I know everything will be all right with all of them. But God, I'm concerned about my work. I'm concerned that

I haven't done all the work that you told me to do." Then, I paused and asked Him, "Have I done the work?"

That was the thought that battled in my mind as I slipped in and out of consciousness. I was drowsy from all the medication that I was taking. However, whenever I was awake, I asked God if I had done the work.

One night, I was only half awake when about three o'clock in the morning, my husband crept into the bedroom where I was quarantined. He did this every night, but on this night, he had his prayer shawl and he threw it over my entire body. He prayed and then, he walked out of the room.

When he left me alone, I felt as if I slipped into a supernatural trance. I knew where I was, I knew I was in the bed, but it was as if I'd entered the spirit realm. I woke up in that realm and found myself wrestling with a spirit. We were pushing and pulling and tugging and pressing; we were in a physical fight.

As I grabbed the spirit, it began to lose its grip on me. Finally, it loosed me and then ran. I knew that spirit had left me completely and I knew why. My husband had thrown his prayer shawl over me—that spirit had to go.

However, the spirit of Covid still remained and a few nights later as I laid in bed, I reached for my phone. I wanted to listen to evangelists on YouTube. I listened to a few before I heard a still voice: *Listen to Reinhard Bonnke.*

It was interesting that I was being told that because I knew he'd died a year before. Still, I obeyed God and began looking up Reinhard Bonnke. In just a few minutes, I came across a sermon of his when Reinhard was preaching in Africa. As I pulled it up, I heard Reinhard talking about the kingdom of God and his voice was filled with such passion.

I said to God, "Why do you have me listening to this? I hear him, but Reinhard isn't praying for anyone."

God said, "*Listen!*"

I kept listening, then at the end, Reinhard said, "I want to pray for everyone who is sick. If anyone is sick, I want you to stand up."

God had told me to listen and now Reinhard was telling me to stand. With the little strength that I had, I rolled out of the bed, pushed myself up, and stood.

Then, Reinhard said, "Now take your hands and place them over the part of your body where you're sick."

When he said that, I told God, "I don't have enough hands." Still, I placed one hand on my chest and I placed one hand on my kidneys because those organs were my chief concern at that point.

As I held my hands in place, Reinhard prayed. Then, he said, "Now, I want you to do something that you couldn't do before this prayer."

I thought for a moment, and then, I focused on my chest. I inhaled, trying to take the deepest breath I possibly could. Then, I exhaled….and it felt as if a thousand razor blades were slicing through my lungs. It was so painful, I could barely stand.

Reinhard repeated his command. "Do something that you could not do before this prayer!"

Even though I was in such pain from the last breath, I tried it again. I inhaled...and the same thing happened. I was attacked by razor blades.

Reinhard said, "Now rejoice if you know you've been healed." Those razor blades were still inside of me, but still, I thanked God for my healing. I hadn't felt the relief yet, but when I laid back down, I knew the hands of God were upon me.

Within a day or two, I felt God's mending beginning. It was like He was putting everything back in place. I was being supernaturally healed from Covid.

After being in the bed for seven days, I was healed, just the way that God had healed me and saved me my entire life.

# LESSONS FROM
# MY CHILDREN

Of course, my children were a part of my life from the moment I found out that I was carrying them. However, I wanted to include their stories separately in this book because there has been so much that I learned from having them in my life.

I'll start with my son. I was pregnant with him when, one day, I went to my grandmother's house and my cousin, Verdie Mae Wilkes, was there. When I walked through the door, she took one look at me and said, "You're getting ready to have a boy."

"Really?"

"Yes." She nodded. "But I want you to know that he's going to be very different. He's going to be peculiar, so different that he will stand out."

Everything else that this prophetess had told me in my life had been true, so I believed her. Plus, this is how it was for all the women in my family. None of us had to have sonograms. That was how strong the prophetic voice was in my relatives.

My cousin went on to tell me everything about this little boy that I was going to birth. She prophesied about the favor that would be on his life and I was excited. I believed everything she said was accurate through Christ Jesus. I was about to have a special son.

Months later, I rushed to the hospital when it was time for me to deliver. I'd dilated, but nothing else happened, nothing else moved. I went into labor for twenty-four hours and then, my son went into distress. The medical team had to perform an emergency C-section.

I was sedated—and they lost me for just a few minutes. At that point, the doctors cleared the room; even Marc couldn't stay in there with me. I can't even imagine how scary that was for him, but to God be the glory, I was able to come back.

I gave birth to my beautiful baby boy, Markale, and from the beginning, I could tell he was special, just like my cousin had prophesied. When he was about six or seven years old, I put him in a private Christian school and one day, when he came home, he said, "Mom, I have to show you what I drew."

"Okay," I said, expecting to smile at the drawing of a six-year-old.

When he held up his picture for me to see, I had to pause for a moment. I was blown away. My son had drawn a picture of warfare right on the paper. He had flames bursting through the clouds, planes falling from the sky. There were people fighting and some running. It was a complete pictorial view of Revelations.

If I hadn't been a Christian, I may not have realized what I was looking at. If my cousin hadn't told me, I may not have realized just how special Markale was.

That was just the beginning. When my son was about six years old, he started having trouble sleeping at night. I didn't know what was wrong, but then, one day he told me, "Mom, every night a man comes and takes me out my room." He took me into his room to show me a small dot that he'd drawn on the wall with a pencil. "See that dot. That's where I go out every night." My son told me this over and over.

At the time, I was still young in my walk and didn't understand what Markale was telling me. I didn't understand the authority that had been placed in me. So, I reached out and asked my spiritual mother to come over and talk to him.

When she arrived, my son looked up at her and said, "Hi, Pastor Dillard."

She said, "Hi, Markale."

He said, "I've got to tell you something."

"What?"

"I was with Jesus last night."

My mouth dropped open, but the Apostle kept talking to him like this was a regular conversation.

"You were with Jesus?" she asked him.

"Yes," my son said. "We went to the water and then we stood on the water. And you know what?"

"What?"

"There were a lot of crabs in the water, but none of the crabs bit me. We just went to the water, just me and Jesus."

Tears rolled down my face as I looked at my baby sharing his experience so innocently. Had this really been happening? Who had been coming to get my son every night?

There was no fear in Markale as he spoke. He recalled his nightly journeys with this man, although this was the first time that he'd called the man Jesus.

As I was listening to my son speak, I reflected once again on what had been prophesied to me before my son was born. Everything she'd said had come true. My son had come into the world with a heart of gold; he wouldn't hurt anybody, not even a fly. He wouldn't even swat at a fly. He was just a gentle young man.

Time moved on and my son graduated from high school when he was sixteen. Since he was so young, he didn't have plans for college at that time, but when he turned seventeen, he said, "Mom, I've always wanted to be a Marine."

The prophetic word had been spoken over his life from the beginning and because of that, I was really leery about him going into the Marines. I hadn't heard a lot of good things about that branch of the military and so, my husband and I were faced with the dilemma of signing the paperwork for him to go.

My son was so excited, though. He was an ROTC child, having taken that in high school, and we didn't want to crush his dreams. So even with all of my anxiety, we signed the papers. However, I could do that because there was one thing I knew—I knew there would be angels with him on assignment.

About a year later, my son went off for training, but just about four weeks later, I received a phone call that my son was being sent home. The Marines had done another medical exam and they'd found a "glitch" in one of his ears.

A few weeks later, my son returned home, totally devastated from losing his dream. He was coming back without a plan B. Once he'd been accepted in the Marines, there hadn't been a need for an alternative plan.

When Markale came home, the assassin went straight into attack mode, wanting to fill him with depression. However, my son fought through it and when he was nineteen, he said, "Okay, Mom, you're a firefighter, so I want to go to school to do that."

I was pleased that he'd found something else of interest. He enrolled to become an EMT and he entered the academy. Markale worked hard, doing everything he needed to do, educating himself to get prepared, so I was shocked when he called me one day at work.

"Mom," he said. "I'm at the doctor's office and I can't see." I said, "What do you mean you can't see?"

What he was saying wasn't making any sense to me. My son was a health nut, always working out; he was in excellent shape and he certainly didn't have any problems with his eyes.

He repeated, "I can't see. The doctor wants me to go straight to the emergency room, but I'm going to drive home."

"No!" I said, trying hard to stay calm. Hadn't my son just told me that he couldn't see? "Stay where you are. Do not drive."

"Mom, I'm just going to Dad's house."

I was so panicked. Markale's words scared me, but still weren't registering. I told my supervisor I had to go and I drove from Pompano Beach to Davie, which was about thirty-five minutes.

When I got to my ex-husband's house, his wife opened the door. "Where's my son?"

"Over there." She pointed to the corner where Markale sat.

I rushed to the corner where he sat, and I gasped. My son didn't even look like himself. He looked more like the Grim Reaper with the way his face was drawn in and his eye were bulging out.

All I could do was say, "Father, you cannot take my son."

I grabbed Markale and helped him walk outside to the car. As I drove, tears rolled down my face and I started to pray. However, I was so distraught from seeing my son, that my prayers were hardly coming out.

I knew what kind of attack this was, though, and I knew that the assassin was aware that I recognized him now. So because I was aware and had grown so strong in my faith, the enemy's attacks were now directed toward my children. The assassin couldn't kill me, so he touched my son.

As we drove, Markale said, "Mom, don't cry. It's going to be all right."

I couldn't stop crying, though, because when I looked at my son, I saw death all over him. I pressed my foot against the gas and sped to the hospital. I drove from Davie to Coral Springs, speaking in tongues the whole way.

When I got to the hospital, Markale could barely move. He was frail and his skin looked gray. I almost carried him into the hospital. When we stumbled through the door, I was met by another Destiny Helper.

My friend, Samantha Washington saw me. At first, she smiled with recognition, but then, she took one look at my son. "Is that Markale?" When I nodded, she said, "Let me take him back immediately."

Back in the emergency room, they got to work on Markale right away, first hooking him up to an IV, and then running tests, trying to determine what was causing his condition.

A couple of hours later, I was bombarded with questions by a nurse. "Was he a diabetic as a child?"

"No!"

"Has he always been sickly?"

"He's never been sick!"

The nurse shook her head as if my answers were hard to believe. "Well, his glucose is over 800. Had you not gotten him here, he would have been dead. But he's here now, and we're going to do everything we can to save him."

Those words rocked me and I sat in the emergency room, praying. How could this be? How could my son have diabetes when he had been fine his whole life? I told God, "You cannot take back what You said…You said he was going to be a peculiar child. You said he was going to be special in your sight."

After several hours, the doctors were able to stabilize him and then, they moved him from the emergency room into intensive care. I sat there in that ICU with Markel for three days, and all I did was pray and rock. I prayed to God asking Him to do what I knew He could do. I knew He could heal because that's what He was—a healer. He was Jehovah Rapha.

As I sat there and prayed, I watched as God answered every one of my prayers. On that first day, his color come back to his body. On the second day his strength came back a little. And then, on the third day, he was ready to walk out of the ICU.

The nurse told me, "We don't normally release a patient from the intensive care unit to his home, but your son is doing so well. We're going to try to get the doctors to sign the orders, to just release him to go home."

I sat there, reflecting on that number three: Father, Son, and the Holy Ghost, meaning it is finished. God gave me the miracle I prayed for.

The lesson in my son's life was that when the assassin couldn't get to me, he sought out my heart. The assassin found who I loved and he wanted to devour Markale to destroy me. This is a lesson for all of us.

A lot of things that happen in your life will not happen directly to you. The attack may go to someone else, but there is no doubt it's all about you.

In my case the assassin said, "Let me take her son out because then, she'll be so broken, she won't be able to operate in the gifts that God has given her. She won't be able to even minister." The assassin knew I wouldn't be able to function if I had lost my son.

However, God wasn't going to allow me to go through this alone. Not only was He there, but on earth, He made sure that I had a Destiny Helper in the form of my friend. Even the nurses were like angels on assignment.

The assassin did not win, but that doesn't mean that the assassin will ever stop trying.

A couple of years later, I was pregnant again. Like before, my cousin spoke a prophecy over me. "You're going to have a girl."

I was pleased with that, and like my son, I knew my daughter would be gifted by God. The Lord had already invested in their gifts; both of them had the grace of their anointing.

However, I also knew that just like with me, just like with my son, the enemy was prepared to go after my daughter. There would be an assassin assigned to my child's demise.

We must have that understanding that the enemy will be there to try to take control of our children and as parents, we sometimes make it easy for the assassin. Sometimes, we open doors in our lives and we do things that go against the Word of God before we come into the knowledge of who we are in the Lord.

However, even once we gain spiritual wisdom, the doors have already been opened and the enemy will attach himself to your children. This saying—what goes around comes around—is not scriptural in itself, but it is true that what you put out will come back to you. You may put out things and never see them come back upon you, but trust me, your children will see it.

For example, if you are promiscuous or you deal with perversion, or you find yourself participating in things that are unnatural, you will look at your son or your daughter and feel like you're looking in the mirror. Those doors that you opened, you never closed and you will find your children living with the mistakes of your past. Often, you will see this with a parent who has a spirit of addiction and then, their child will have the same addiction. Those generational curses haven't been broken, the doors haven't been closed to the enemy. Now the assassin that was assigned to the adult becomes attached to the child. As my daughter was growing up, I saw this happening a bit with me and my beautiful baby girl.

Again, carrying her was a difficult pregnancy—I busted blood vessels trying to give birth to her—but once she was here, I was so happy. I had a little girl in my life, Imani, and I couldn't wait to raise her. My plan had been to raise her better than I'd been raised, but I ended up raising her the same way—materialistically. I dressed her up like a baby doll, making sure she had the best clothes and her hair was always perfect. I made sure that every day she looked like she was on a magazine cover.

I did this because, just like my mother wanted for me, I wanted my daughter to have better than what I had.

However, as Imani grew up, I looked at my little girl, and it was as if I was looking into a mirror. So much of who I was, I created in her. She was beautiful, but she was a little selfish and a bit self-centered. That came from how I raised her, how I treated her, how I tried to mold her.

Everything I did, I did because I loved her and that meant that I had to protect her, too. I'd been molested as a child, so I had both the natural gates and the spiritual gates around her regarding that closed tightly. I made sure Imani would never suffer the way I had.

The challenge with that was, while I had my eyes on those gates and kept those gates closed, I left other gates open. Because I had a bit of tunnel vision in this aspect, I had to watch my daughter go through so many things I'd gone through.

When she was in high school, I watched that same spirit of jealousy follow her. She had the same challenges with girls who didn't like her, girls who wanted to fight her. Just like I had to fight just for being who God wanted me to be, she had to do the same. She had to fight the same battles that I'd already been through it.

The enemy kept coming after Imani using my weaknesses.

One day when my daughter was in high school, I came home from work and as soon as I walked into the house, I said to myself—who has been in my house?

My daughter was home, so I went to her. I stood in the door to her bedroom and stared at her for a moment before I said, "Somebody has been in my house."

Of course, she didn't want to get in trouble, so she said, "Nobody's been in your house."

I didn't say anything else, just turned around and left her in her room. However, that wasn't the end for me. I went into my kitchen and then, took a slow stroll through the room, looking around, checking everything. I was keen in the spirit and God had given me discernment over my atmosphere. Something was off—I knew it. It took me a few minutes, but finally, I saw crumbs on the counter.

I marched right back into Imani's room. "Who's been in my house?"

Again, she told me the same thing. "Nobody's been in your house."

I didn't say anything about the crumbs. I just went into my bedroom and began to pray. I'd already had these same battles with the spirit of perversion and the spirit of fornication. Now, they were attaching themselves to my daughter.

Since I didn't believe Imani was telling me the truth, I asked God. "What's been going on in my home?" I prayed.

God revealed that there had been a young man in my house. I didn't realize that my daughter was already in these battles. How could she be? She was only fourteen!

I was devastated. The enemy hadn't been able to kill me so he was coming for my daughter, who was predestined to be a prophetess. I was sick when the Holy Ghost showed me what had been happening with her.

Now, I was raging with anger, but I wasn't angry with Imani. I had learned to remove the face so that I could see the enemy, see the assassin.

I had to understand that with my daughter, I was looking in the mirror. Not only with the assassin, but with so many of the good things that she was doing, too. I'd opened up my first business when I was twenty-three; my daughter opened up her first business when she was seventeen—the same type of business with hair. I loved designer clothes and my daughter's taste was expensive just like mine…actually her taste was one-hundred times worse. It was as if my child was a replica of me. My daughter had taken both the good and the bad and taken them to a higher and greater level.

When speaking with my children, I often found myself saying, "No, don't go this way. I've been there before." But of course, children must chart their own course, they must choose their own road to travel. There is nothing we can do to stop them from having to face the enemy. All we can do is prepare them and then cancel the assignments through our prayers.

—⊶⊙⁊

One day, my daughter came to me and told me she was having challenges with her business. Every time she started making a certain amount of money, there seemed to be something always pulling her back.

Her words surprised me; I didn't know that Imani had been going through all of this. After we spoke, the Lord gave me a revelation through a dream.

Imani was having hair sent to me and I was sitting and waiting for the FedEx guy with my delivery . When the box arrived, the person put the box on the counter. But before I could get up and reach for my package, a demonic spirit appeared, grabbed my package and ran away with it. I tried to chase this demon who'd taken my package, but I couldn't catch him.

God interpreted the dream for me. *"Demons are stealing your daughter's products and attacking her finances. They were there to destroy her business, they were there to destroy her destiny."*

Once I had that revelation, I again came to understand just how similar our lives were. Watching Imani reminded me of my struggles with my business. It was as if I'd made footprints and my daughter was stepping into the same footprints. I hated that now, she was struggling, too.

When I'd made those footprints, I wasn't where I was now in Christ. Now, I was spiritually awakened, so with Imani, I knew what I had to do. I had to stir up the sand and change those footprints. That was when I got down on my knees and prayed that my daughter would make her own prints and not follow in mine. My prayer for her was that her footprints would be on the right track, and on her track, God would make every crooked way straight for her.

My prayers for my daughter have been working. My daughter is gifted in the prophetic and she has confessed Christ as her Savior. She is growing into that every day, continuing to learn how to defeat the enemy. Her fight, and my son's fight, seems to be much greater than mine. The enemy has attacked them since they're both spiritually gifted. However on the other hand, they are called, they are anointed and their favor is greater, too. So they will be able to walk in boldness and be fearless—because of their gifts and the favor of God.

Even with all of that, still, my children need my backup. As parents, we are spiritually awakened, so we are our children's reinforcements, we are the righteous prayers that they need.

There is one thing that I know for sure…there is nothing like the prayers of a mother. And a mother and a father will never stop when it comes to their children. Even when we see change, we'll keep going, we'll keep praying. Covering our children with prayer should never stop.

I know the importance of having the prayers of the righteous in my life. After my mom passed away, if it had not been for Apostle Janice Dillard stepping into the role of my spiritual mother and praying for me, I would have been dead.

Now that I've benefitted from what God gave to me, I must be that Destiny Helper and that spiritual mother. Of course Markale and Imani are my biological children, but I cannot be just their mother alone because a child is only of a few days. So I move from mother to spiritual mother. We must all do that for our children.

The more we seek God, the more He will give us the tools, the wisdom, the knowledge and the understanding to come up against the adversary. Not one of our children has to be lost because now, we know.

We must become obedient protectors of our children, through the word of God. It's like the story of Jericho. The Israelites were told to walk silently around the walls of Jericho once, every day for six days. On the seventh day, they were to walk around seven times, then sound the alarm, and the walls of the city would fall.

The Israelites had to put in the work for those six days, just like we know there's work we must do over our children. There will come a day, however, when we will sound that alarm and every tactic of the enemy will have to come down.

We just have to understand that God will allow some things to form, God will allow some things to happen. We cannot stop that. We cannot give our children total protection, even if we want to. However, we also must know that when we need the plans that have been formed against our children to be destroyed, it will all come down.

Knowing that our children will have to go through some things is hard for a parent to accept. There will be times when you will have to stand back. You'll see something happening and you'll want to attack it to save your child. However, just because you see it, doesn't mean you must attack it. You must remember that there is always a proper time.

Take the time to study your opponent, you must study the assassin. You cannot ever move prematurely because if you do, you'll be in a reactionary mode, moving on your emotions. You never want to be in a situation where you're just reacting because your emotional reaction could drive your child into the arms of the assassin. As you pray God will tell you when to move. Then, and only then should you go on the attack.

By that point, you will have all the information you need about what's going on with your child, you will have had time to plan your strategy and you will be ready to go!

Again, I want to repeat that I know it will be hard to stand back when you see something going on with your child. Especially when you see them going through something that you've been through already. You'll want to grab your child and just shake them. Just remember, you cannot make any premature moves. Always be mindful, always be aware, always be careful not to do anything to push our children into the arms of the enemy. It is also important to remember Proverbs 22:6: *Train up a child in the way he should go. Even when he grows older, he will not abandon it.* You must trust the way you've raised your children, but most importantly, you must trust God.

# MY PRAYER FOR YOU

Father, in the mighty and matchless name of Jesus with humility, I come before the throne of grace with a transparent, and repented heart. I apostolically and prophetically release Divine Helpers, who have charge over your life, that they will gird the gates and protect your spiritual investments. I activate the angelic hosts and command them to move on your behalf and on the behalf of every reader. Reveal purpose, call, and destiny, Father, awaken every spiritual sense. Arise and let the assassin be scattered. Father, we come in the volume of the book through glorious riches, and by faith our hidden treasures are revealed.

Jesus, you are the Deliverer and in 1 John 4:4: and our salvation is found in your sacrifice. In John 10:9-11, Father, you died so that we would no longer fall victim to the assassin or be bound by fear, ignorance, or distorted thoughts.

I speak an atmosphere of possibilities into your life, knowing that with God, all things are possible. I decree and declare that every process was necessary for God's divine agenda in your life.

I salute you and stand as a mouthpiece and ambassador, knowing that He is the one who completed everything before we stepped into a moment of time. I pray this prayer will reach the nations and stir up your spirit and expedite you to your destiny place. I pray the light of the world will be turned on by the power source, which is Jesus Christ. I release a fire of the Holy Ghost that the glory will be refined for your destiny.

I pray that there is an interruption of any activity that the assassin has started in your life that will hijack your purpose and the plan that God has for you. I release apostolic authority over your region, that you will be activated in the realm of the spirit. I pray that you will be revived, realigned and resuscitated and that will bring revival to your house.

I pray that these words will catapult you to your destiny, but Love, I pray that the Lord will fortify you, that you will be graced in His love and that you will be covered in the precious name of Jesus. And every spiritual gift will be awakened.

Amen.

# About the Author

Prophetess Kayle Washington Bryant is a much sought after talk show host, conference speaker, and preacher. She co-pastors Apostle Faith Church of Jesus in Ft. Lauderdale, Florida, with her husband, Bishop Clarence Joseph Bryant. Her life experiences and spiritual testimonies give her an ability to release the apostolic prophetic anointing into the lives of God's people, birthing deliverance to the body of Christ. She attended various colleges, earning her Bachelor's of Religious in Biblical Studies.

Currently, Prophetess Bryant is the show host of *It Happened, You Saw It, You Are Not Crazy* featured on the Wynn Network.

Made in the USA
Columbia, SC
15 October 2021